# NOTES OF A CRUISE

IN THE

# WESTERN PACIFIC.

# NOTES OF A CRUISE

## IN H.M.S. "FAWN"

IN THE

# WESTERN PACIFIC

IN THE YEAR 1862.

BY

T. H. HOOD.

**Rediscovery Books**

Reproduced by kind permission of the
Royal Geographical Society

Published by

**Rediscovery Books Ltd**

Unit 10, Ridgewood Industrial Park,

Uckfield, East Sussex,

TN22 5QE England

Tel: +44 (0) 1825 749494

Fax: +44 (0) 1825 765701



To find out more about Rediscovery Books

and its range of titles visit

**www.rediscoverybooks.com**

Published in association with

The **Royal Geographical Society with IBG** was founded in 1830 to advance geographical science. Today it supports geographical research, promotes geography in schools and through outdoor learning, in society and to policy makers. Geography connects us to the world's people, places and environments.

The **Rediscovery Books** series allow us to see how previous geographers and travellers understood and recorded the world.

*In reprinting in facsimile from the original, any imperfections are inevitably reproduced and the quality may fall short of modern type and cartographic standards.*

Fr a Photog. by Commander R.P. Cator R.N. W. & A.K. Johnston, Edinr.

HOUSE AT FALEASAU

Edmonston & Douglas

# CONTENTS.

## CHAPTER I.

### TO AUCKLAND.



## CHAPTER II.

### NIUE.



## CHAPTER III.

### PASSAGE TO SAMOA.

## CHAPTER IV.

### PASSAGE TO TUTUILA.



## CHAPTER V.

### PAGO-PAGO.



## CHAPTER VI.

### UPOLU—APIA.



## CHAPTER VII.

### UPOLU.

## CHAPTER VIII.

UPOLU—TUTUILA.



## CHAPTER IX.

TUTUILA.



## CHAPTER X.

SAVAII.



## CHAPTER XI.

SAMOA.

## CHAPTER XII.

UEA.



## CHAPTER XIII.

MOA.



## CHAPTER XIV.

OFF FIJI.



## CHAPTER XV.

KUNAIE, OR THE ISLE OF PINES.

## CHAPTER XVI.

### NORFOLK ISLAND.



## APPENDIX.

# LIST OF ILLUSTRATIONS.

# CRUISE OF THE "FAWN."

## CHAPTER I.

### TO AUCKLAND.

As H.M.S. "Fawn" steamed out of Sydney harbour at 2 P.M. on Wednesday, 7th May, it rained heavily, and the wind came down in strong squalls, promising us anything but a pleasant commencement of our voyage to the islands of the Western Pacific. We were, however, agreeably disappointed, and had smooth seas and bright summer skies to the north cape of New Zealand. On the 12th we sighted the remarkable rock in mid ocean called Ball's Pyramid, 1800 feet in height, and on the following morning, Lord Howe's Island, where we were becalmed two days. One or two large sharks were captured, and suffered death in a manner no other creature would be subjected to at the hands of English sailors, whose usual tenderness for animals is (not without some reason) utterly wanting in respect to the tiger of the sea.

Almost every one who has seen much of salt water has some anecdote or other to tell about a shark; but the adventure that befel the gunner of the "Fawn" was more than usually strange. Being a very expert diver, he had been employed to recover the treasure from the Peninsular and Oriental Company's ship "Ava," wrecked a few years ago on the coast of Ceylon. Having, in a gutta-percha dress, made his way into the saloon, he was busy searching for the bullion, when, to his horror, he saw a huge ground-shark come sailing in at the door. With great presence of mind he lay motionless on the locker, and watched it silently and grimly cruising about. One can well imagine his feelings when he saw its cold green eyes fixed upon him, and felt it pushing against the leaden soles of his boots, and rubbing against his dress, the slightest puncture in which would have been certain destruction. After ten minutes of suspense, which must have seemed an age, during which the monster came back twice or thrice to have another look at him, Mr. Pounds' courage and coolness were rewarded by seeing him steering his way back as he came.

Afterwards he always armed himself with a large dagger when he went down to the wreck, from which he recovered altogether £220,000, having spent 850 hours under water. He had also some narrow escapes at times, from the opening and shutting of the iron plates of the ship as they worked with the roll of the sea. The air-pipe was twice severed from his helmet; but fortunately slackening, it warned the people above to lose no time in rescuing him from his perilous position.

From the Cape to Auckland we had a slight experience of New Zealand winter weather, and beat up yesterday to the harbour, across Hauraki Gulf, against a strong south-wester, cold enough to reduce the thermometer to 43°. We found all quiet here, the Maories being at present kept in good humour by the conciliatory policy of Sir George Grey. To many, the concessions made may seem too great; but if a good military road is pushed meantime across the island, and a chain of forts established, Sir George's policy may possibly hereafter be acknowledged to have been a wise and humane one.

On every side, in approaching Auckland, one sees evidences of the volcanic disturbances which have given its peculiar aspect to the scenery. On one side of the entrance is the truncated cone of Rangitoto; and behind the town, conspicuous amongst the many similar small ones, is that of Mount Eden, the crater of which is very perfect. Nearly all these cones, which have covered the plains between the Manukau and Auckland waters with scoriæ, are scarped in parallel terraces, having been fortified "Pahs" in times not long gone by, when fierce wars were waged between the various tribes (those *horrida bella*), when the victors feasted upon the bodies of the vanquished.

Notwithstanding their having been so lately addicted to cannibalism, the Maories are a fine race; and it is to be regretted that we had not contented ourselves with civilizing the northern island by means of "the Book," instead of colonizing it at the point of the sword.

The amount of really valuable land is limited in proportion to the area, and there is no great prospect of its having any considerable export, like the middle island, unless indeed the gold fields should prove rich. At present there is considerable excitement regarding that of Coromandel. I had not an opportunity of visiting it; but from all accounts, it does not seem probable that it will be a remunerative field to the common digger, although companies may obtain good returns for the employment of capital upon the quartz reefs. Should it turn out what the Australians call a "poor man's diggings," there is likely to be some trouble with the native owners of the soil, who have already refused £10,000, offered to them by the Colonial Government, in addition to a fee of £1, to be paid by each digger.

Auckland is not a very interesting place; were it not for the Maories, it would be dull indeed. At present the traders in the place are thriving upon the large Government expenditure, there being five thousand troops of the line in the province, chiefly employed in constructing the road towards the Waikato country.

The neighbourhood of the town looks bare, there being no timber nearer than the kauri forest on the hills, eight miles away; the blue gums, poplars, and other trees not yet having grown sufficiently to give a shaded appearance to the plain, and, unless planted in large masses, it is doubtful whether the fierce winds, which sweep over the level between the waters of the Manukau harbour and those of the eastern coast, will permit them to attain to a size sufficient to give a clothed look to the district, at one time covered with the noble kauri, which when once destroyed, by fire or otherwise, seems never to spring again, as is the case with the forests of black pine and totara on the plains of Canterbury. Amongst the trees lately introduced, the beautiful Norfolk Island pine is the most conspicuous for luxuriance of growth.

Few of the fields are fenced with hedge-rows, which already give an English aspect to some of the other settled parts of New Zealand, especially to the plains around Christ Church, in the province of Canterbury. Here they are enclosed with walls of scoria, which the farmer must gather from the surface of the ground before commencing to plough; but when once brought into cultivation the pulverized volcanic ashes make a most fertile soil, and the verdure and rich appearance of the grass equals that of the old pastures in England. Some of the farms of the pensioners in the vicinity between Otahu and Onahunga, in sequestered nooks and corners, are pretty and comfortable looking. Further on, advancing into the Waikato country, the scenery improves much in luxuriance and beauty.

A few hours after we anchored in the Waltemata's "glittering waters," as its name implies, there was a severe thunderstorm, and the ground was covered, to the depth of some inches, with hailstones. This is an unusual occurrence here; and in the middle island, on the great plains on the eastern sides of the Cordillera, thunderstorms are almost as seldom experienced as on the low lands of Peru under the heights of the Andes.

I had the pleasure to-day of meeting at the hotel one of the chiefs of the Ahuriri Province, who, although unable to speak English, in manners, dress, and appearance looked a thorough gentleman. He gave me an invitation to come and pay him a visit, promising to escort me to the Phlegræan fields around Taupo and Rotumahana lakes, where, in addition to other most interesting objects to a geologist or lover of nature, are to be seen geysers scarcely inferior in beauty and grandeur to those of Iceland. Some day I hope still to see the smoke ascending from the neighbouring volcano of Tongoriro, and to shoot the rapids of the Waikato river in a canoe manned by thirty or forty Maori rowers, when the dwellers by its banks have ceased to think of possible war with "the Pakehah."

Having no intention of making a book, I shall leave those who may take the trouble to read these notes to obtain information regarding this interesting country from the hundred volumes[1] already published, especially referring them to the works of Dr. Thomson and the Rev. Mr. Taylor, contenting myself with giving such information as I may be able to gather respecting the more remote and less known islands we are bound for.

[1] See APPENDIX.

## CHAPTER II.

### NIUE.

22*d May.*—We left Auckland this afternoon, and floated quietly down with the tide into Hauraki Gulf; our destination being, in the first place, Niue or Savage Island, regarding which little appears to be known. When that great navigator and most correct observer, Captain Cook, discovered it, he succeeded as usual in landing, but did not manage to hold the slightest communication with the natives, who came down, he said, with the ferocity of "wild boars." Hence the name he bestowed upon their island, which, by all accounts, it still deserves, although Captain (now Admiral) Erskine, who visited it in H.M.S. "Havannah" in 1849, but could not land, in consequence of the heavy swell, reports more favourably regarding the natives. Since then more than one of Her Majesty's ships have been off the coast, but no report has been received, so far as we have learned, of any improvement having taken place in their disposition.

*4th June.*—We sighted Niue this afternoon, and are now standing off and on until the morning. Our passage from New Zealand has been agreeable, and the weather generally has been fine, with a high barometer. On the 25th and 26th May, we saw much sea-weed floating; on the following day none was visible, as we apparently had crossed the current which bore it, in all probability, from the East Cape. On the 28th and 29th, in latitude 28°, west longitude 168°, we encountered a pretty stiff gale from the north-east, with heavy rain. The barometer did not fall lower than 29·90, and on the 1st of June, when we may consider that we had the regular trade-wind carrying us before it, it was at 30·33. We observed no albatrosses after the 2d, when the last large white-backed one bade us adieu, the Cape pigeons having turned back on the previous day. One or two boatswain-birds and gannets have been seen during the last day or two, but the ocean is very solitary here; no sails have been seen, nor have we observed a single whale. Every one is looking forward to our visit to this island to-morrow, when, as it is Captain Cator's intention to land if possible, we hope to have the satisfaction of being perhaps the first Europeans who have seen anything of Niue.

*5th June.*—A hot cloudy morning and threatening showers flying about. At half-past 10 o'clock we stood in within four miles of the land, when we saw the canoes of the natives paddling towards us. They soon came alongside, but as we were going fast through the water, the first two or three failed to catch the ropes thrown to them. Not in the least disconcerted, their merry-looking crews of four in each boat plied their paddles lustily, and, although we were going six knots, did not drop much astern. Sail having been shortened, the next canoe succeeded in getting hold of the line, and one of the men, taking off his mat, rolled it round in a plantain leaf, and, with a net in his teeth, plunged into the water, and came up under the taffrail, calling out, to our surprise, "You fliend Engleez; give rope, all right!" He soon came up on the loose line thrown to him, hand over hand, and made his appearance on deck decently attired in a clean fringed mat. He was followed by another, who, not so particular, came up with his kilt of green leaves of the Dracœna, all dripping, looking like a veritable son of the sea-god. They were quickly succeeded by numbers, and we had before long eighteen to twenty canoes alongside with pigs, plantains, bananas, malay-apples, cocoa-nuts, spears, and other articles of commerce. They seemed very anxious to trade, and had their little shops all along the deck. We soon found they had a "pretty smart" idea of the value of a "tanna," as they had learned to call a shilling, and of doing business, gained, no doubt, by their intercourse with whalers, sailing under the "stars and stripes," which we found were now constantly in the habit of coming here for supplies.

Instead of the uncouth ferocious savages we had expected, we found them pleasant, good-looking fellows, of a light olive complexion, with well-shaped features, clean, quite sufficiently attired for the climate, very merry and happy, but quiet, and remarkably well behaved. The younger men were ready for any "lark," as the sailors said, and after being decorated in fantastic style in the forecastle, with red and green paint (for which the artists were paid liberally with shells and bananas) some of them danced with great glee, and in good time, to the jigs and hornpipes played by the ship's musician.

The only *faux pas* I observed committed was by one who, having obtained possession of a marine's old scarlet jacket in exchange for his goods, had struggled into it as a pair of breeches, and came ignominiously upon his back on the quarter-deck. He heartily enjoyed the absurdity of his position, from which four stout fellows extricated him with some difficulty amid shouts of laughter.

Bright cotton handkerchiefs, fish-hooks, knives, and trousers, seemed most prized; and many were the inquiries made for Jews' harps, of which, unfortunately, we had none on board. Amongst others, a Samoan teacher came on board, and from him, to our pleasure and surprise, we heard that there was an English missionary residing in the next bay. The first native who had come on board, putting his hands together in the attitude of prayer, and looking up to heaven, had given us to understand that there was a missionary on the island, who, we concluded, must be a Samoan teacher.

We went round to make certain; and steam having now been got up, and the sails all furled, as soon as the screw began to move, whether from astonishment and alarm (though they had been previously warned by Sioele the Samoan), or because they did not like going beyond the limits of their own village shore, a large number of our visitors jumped overboard with their goods, and coming up to the surface of the water with them, held high in one hand, swam off with ease to their canoes.

They are splendid swimmers; but strange to say, small as the island is, twelve miles by eight, there are, we were told, villages in the interior, whose inhabitants have never been to the sea-shore, and who are laughed at by their neighbours for their inability to swim.

On rounding the little promontory dividing the bay of Avatele, off which we had been, we came in sight of the settlement of Alofi; conspicuous by the white cottage and church of the mission. No doubt, the native who saluted Captain Erskine with "Alofa" so importunately, and appeared to him to be praying, wished to make him understand that there was a teacher at this place. The cutter was soon lowered, and as we pulled ashore, we met a canoe bringing off a letter to Captain Cator from the Rev. Mr. Lawes. The tide being high we could not pull close in shore, but were met at the edge of the reef by a number of stalwart fellows, who, after a general hand-shaking, informed us they were our friends, and proved themselves such, by carrying us ashore on their shoulders. My bearer tramped along at a capital pace, considering his rider's weight, and actually ran over the sharp coral with his bare feet. On reaching the white sandy beach, we shook hands with the crowd of men, women, and children, who gave us the warmest welcome, with the exception of a few of the last generation, who, sitting on a bank, appeared to take little notice of us. All appeared quite delighted with the excitement of such a large party of Papalangis arriving to visit their missionary, Mr. Lawes, who was heartily glad to see his countrymen. He came out from England ten months ago with his young wife, to take charge of this isolated mission. Fortunately, all has gone well, and the people have behaved kindly, indeed, almost affectionately to them. All honour to the brave man who ventured upon such an undertaking, and to his even more courageous wife. The natives had, previous to their arrival, built a most excellent house, eighty feet long, with verandah and venetians, much nicer looking, and better adapted to the climate than the uninteresting-looking edifices of the settlers in tropical Australia; and this they erected under the directions of the Samoan teachers, who are entitled to the great merit of civilizing the savage islanders.

The roof inside is quite an elaborate work of art; the thatch, neatly stitched down upon battens closely laid together, resting upon round rafters, most ingeniously fitted, has a very pleasing effect.

Not a single nail is used in the building, everything being tied with cocoa-nut sinnet. The rooms are divided by thick walls six feet high, without ceilings, so that from each the whole of the ornamental roof is visible. They had just finished and presented to Mr. Lawes a sofa nicely made, and inlaid with quaint imitations of birds and fishes in tortoise-shell and mother-of-pearl.

The church, built in the same manner, can accommodate from six to eight hundred people, and is crowded every Sunday. The supporting central posts of both buildings are large trees, of a wood resembling mahogany in grain (*Calophyllum Inophyllum*), about twenty-five to thirty feet in length, and were conveyed twelve miles upon men's shoulders, along the winding shore.

There are five other principal villages : Avatele and Makufu to the south ; Mutalau on the south-west; and Liku on the eastern side; at each of which there is a missionary station, and resident Samoan teachers. At Avatele the church is larger and more elaborately ornamented than that at Alofi. We saw sitting in Mr. Lawes's room, Paulo, Elia, and Sakaio, thoughtful, contemplative-looking men,—a shade darker in complexion than the generality of the Niuans,—who, with the other Samoans, assisted principally in bringing about the great change that has taken place here since the first teacher landed in 1847. He was a native of the island, educated at the mission establishment at Malua, and at first his life was in great danger, but he persevered in his efforts, and a considerable number of the people had ceased to worship the spirits of their ancestors and the terrible gods of disease; they no longer lay in wait to kill some passing enemy, and they had discontinued to a considerable extent the common crime of infanticide, chiefly practised before birth, when the Samoan teachers arrived among them.

Not only in religious matters had the native missionaries successfully exerted themselves, but in many other ways a great improvement had been effected in the state of the island. Instead of families living in wretched hovels in isolated situations in the bush, they are now collected in villages chiefly around the mission stations. There is a good road all round the coast from village to village, made by convict labour. The chiefs, or rather the heads of families, the form of government being patriarchal, meet together at stated times in each district, and arrange its public affairs. Through their influence the construction of so many fathoms of road has been substituted as a punishment for the old sentence of being tied up without food, eating acrid fruits, and the like. Old and young, men and women, are equally liable to this kind of hard-labour system; and if refractory or lazy, are subjected to the ancient and more disagreeable penalty, of being lashed, hands and feet, to a bamboo for days, sufficient food being given to prevent death from actual starvation. To-morrow, a boy is to undergo this punishment for tatooing himself, a fashion not now approved of by the *haut ton* of Savage Island.

Mr. Lawes has done a great deal since his arrival. He is prime minister, doctor, instructor in divers trades, as well as religious teacher in the island, and both he and his wife appear to have influence. He modestly admitted, however, that the chief merit is due to his Kannaka associates, who had almost finished by themselves a translation of the New Testament into the Niuan dialects, together with hymns which have been completed and printed at Malua.

His wife has twelve handmaidens who all appear very attentive and anxious to please her. Some of them to-day, unable to restrain their curiosity, followed us to the church and other places, along with the crowd of our attendants. When reproved

HEATHEN WARRIOR AND HIS WIFE.

for the neglect of their duties, they were very penitent, and with tears in their eyes said, "Oh yes, we are very bad; send us away, and get good servants." Some of the women are very good-looking; the gentle expression of the nurse's face, no doubt, makes her mistress feel quite safe in intrusting her child to the care of a savage islander, notwithstanding her frizzed-out head of hair, which her charge did not appear much to approve of. Many wore their hair short, but this we found was only a temporary arrangement, as when it has grown to the length of twelve or eighteen inches, it is cut off for the purpose of being plaited into thin braids, a number of which are worn around the waist, and are not always readily parted with, being much prized by the men, who follow the same custom. It is to be presumed they exchange their love-locks, and hence their value.

The children are very apt scholars, and many even of the grown-up men were anxious to show their proficiency in writing; pencils and paper, strange to say, being presents highly esteemed in Niue. They seem an ingenious race of people; and their canoes, which are very nicely carved and ornamented, especially attracted our notice. In appearance, they are certainly much more prepossessing than the Maories, their relatives by one side of the house, the ancestors of both having originally come from Samoa, without a cross of blood probably in the veins of the Niuans, beyond that which marks the difference between the Samoans and Tongans, their more immediate progenitors.

Cannibalism, so far as the missionaries can ascertain, has never been practised here. It seems the more probable that this is the case, seeing that they do not now care much for animal food. When the Samoans first landed, mice were the only quadrupeds; now they have pigs in abundance, but seldom eat them, contenting themselves, when hungry, with bananas, baked taro, or yam, and fish, for the evening meal. They refused tobacco; nor do they indulge in the kava bowl, like most of the Polynesians. It seems that the unenviable sobriquet of Savage Island was obtained in consequence of their killing every stranger who landed, even any of their own countrymen who returned after a lengthened absence, from their superstitious dread of disease. In their intense fear of sickness, they prayed to the dreaded sailing gods to avoid their shores, like the Samoans and other islanders, who, before tasting the cup of ava at evening meal, poured out a libation to their various deities, never forgetting their addresses to these especially: "Here is ava for you. Oh, sailing gods! do not come ashore at this place, but be pleased to depart along the ocean to some other land."

Peinamina, the native teacher before alluded to, narrowly escaped death on this account, his utmost eloquence and powers of reasoning being necessary to persuade his countrymen to spare him for a time, whilst he kept himself away from their neighbourhood, lest he should bear about him any infection. But even this stringent law was not always strictly adhered to. Mr. Lawes was informed by an old native, whom we saw at his house, that he was present when the first white man landed since the time of Cook. It appears that a whaler was lying off the island, and bartering with the natives in their canoes, who were still wild as when first seen. The master, as the ship got under weigh, savagely threw overboard one of his men amongst these supposed cannibals, who however took compassion upon the stranger, saved him from drowning, and took him ashore. A debate ensued as to what was to be done on so unprecedented an occasion. It was evidently not the man's own wish to land upon their shore.

Some stood by the ancient law. Salt water was in his eyes—the mark of shipwreck—he must die. But the majority were against it, and the matter was settled by their giving him a canoe, and supplying him with some bananas and cocoa-nuts; and so they sent him out to sea. After lurking about in caves on the coast for some days, he succeeded in getting on board another whaler cruising in the neighbourhood.

Polygamy is common, but under the influence of the new religion, is decreasing; and the population has risen from 4700 at the present census, taken by the Samoans, to 5000, in consequence of children being all permitted to come into the world alive, and from the better treatment of the mothers afterwards.[1]

The women are modest; infidelity is severely punished; and illegitimate children are always thrown into the sea. Suicide is not unusual; when urged by some violent paroxysm of passion, they rush to the edge of some high coral cliff, and throw themselves down headlong. They are very fond of amusements, and of music. The only instrument we saw was a double flute, like that of the ancient Egyptians, which they play with *the*

[1] See APPENDIX.

*nostrils*, the performer presenting a most grotesque appearance. Wars between the tribes have been of frequent occurrence, even on this small island. Possibly they think it well to keep their hands accustomed to the spear and bow, as they are sometimes threatened with foreign invasion. The Tongans, the modern Danes of the Pacific, whom, although an offshoot themselves from that race, they hate, and call "man-eaters," attempted not very long ago to conquer them. In consequence of their superior weapons and discipline, and perhaps contemptuous daring—for the Tongans are prouder in their way than the Romans of old, or even modern Britons—they were carrying all before them, when they were destroyed by a stratagem. The coast is pierced with deep narrow clefts in the rock; across one of these the Niuans laid light branches, covered with banana and cocoa-nut leaves, with soil over all. The Tongans rushed furiously forward to attack their taunting and now retreating enemies, and, falling headlong into the chasm, were killed in great numbers. The rest were massacred, but not eaten.

Their own dead are generally put into a canoe, and sent adrift; or else the body is laid upon a bier in the woods until the skeleton is bleached, when the bones are placed in family vaults in the limestone.

This island, situated in lat. 19° 8′, and long. 169° 44′ w., is an up-raised coral plateau, nearly of an equal elevation, about 250 feet above the level of the sea in its highest part. Its surface is much fissured, as if its last elevation had been sudden. This seems borne out by the tradition of the natives, who say that when their forefathers, Hunanaki and Fao, landed, having swam there from Tonga, it was just above the waters, and washed by the waves. They stamped upon it, and suddenly it arose from the ocean; a second stamp caused trees and plants to spring, and cover its surface, when they obtained wives for themselves, made from the Ti palm.

The island possesses an equable and healthy climate, is about forty miles in circumference, and well wooded with trees, similar to those found in the adjacent groups. The soil is of no great depth; and although the nuts are remarkably fine, the cocoa-palms are, so far as we saw, small and stunted-looking. Arrow-root can be produced in large quantities; several thousand pounds were obtained last year in payment for Bibles, or rather, for the four Gospels, then published. Wherever the bush is burnt, the cassava plant grows spontaneously.

The supply of water is indifferent, the principal dependence of the inhabitants being on the reservoirs in caves in the coral limestone. In one at Alofi, the missionaries have sunk a deep pit into which the water drops incessantly from the roof, and keeps the reservoir constantly full, which, like most of the similar ones on the island, rises and falls with the tide. It is singular that the supply should be so constant and equal, as there is so little elevation of the land above the roof of the cave, which is about 100 feet above the sea-level. The floor of these caves is thickly incrusted with stalagmite. From this the natives make round balls like grape-shot, which they throw from the hand with deadly precision without a sling.

So far as we could learn, the natural history of Niue possesses no peculiar interest; its fauna and flora being on a limited scale, and similar to those of the larger islands to the north-west. Doves and pigeons abound; and the large cocoa-nut-eating crab (*Birgus latro*) is very common, and highly esteemed as an article of food by the natives. The variety of ferns is great, and some remarkable specimens were obtained during our short visit.

Pleasant surprises are amongst the most agreeable things in life. I don't remember ever being better pleased than with our reception at Savage Island. It was scarcely possible to realize the fact of our being actually there, as we sat round Mr. Lawes's comfortable tea-table, in a well-furnished house.

There being no anchorage, Captain Cator was unable to gratify our entertainer's pressing wish that we should remain another day, which we would all gladly have done, more especially as to-morrow the Niuan "Parliament" is to assemble, and offenders are to be tried and punished. At sunset we reluctantly bade them farewell; and after another general hand-shaking with old and young, who pressed round the boat, some swimming alongside to bid us good-bye, we left the shore of these highly interesting and pleasant people, and their adventurous instructors, in whose future fate we shall all feel an interest, although I entertain no fear for their safety.

We were glad to be able to supply them with late English news, which one can well imagine must be most refreshing to people so isolated from the world. Now and then a whaler calls in and they get some American papers. A few weeks since they obtained a Boston journal, printed in the year of grace 1834, something new, no doubt, in its way. It must be most tantalizing to see, as has happened more than once, ships sailing past without having any communication. More than one of Her Majesty's ships have actually called off the island, and had intercourse with the natives, without being aware that there was even a practicable landing-place. Many of these supposed cannibals wished to come in the ship with us, and so great is the desire among them now to go abroad and see the world, that often, some days after whalers have left the coast, two or three half-starved wretches have made their appearance from the hold, and it is usually almost necessary to use force to make the poor would-be emigrants leave the vessel on its departure from the coast. It is to be feared that this eagerness to emigrate may result in great misery to many islanders, as we have heard a report that the numbers of unhappy wretches, labouring under the direst slavery, in the guano-pits of the Chincha Islands, have been recruited by Polynesians as well as Chinese.

## CHAPTER III.

### PASSAGE TO SAMOA.

*6th June.*—The ship is festooned to-day with bananas, pine-apples, paupaus, and so on, while rows of slaughtered little pigs, the purchases of the sailors, are strung out of sight. It is very hot; for, instead of the trade-wind, which appears of late years to be very uncertain here, we are close-hauled to one from the north-north-east. By the meteorological register kept at Malua, it appears that the south-east trade does not blow there generally more than twenty days in the month, and veers round by north to north-west and south-west. From the north-west it sometimes blows very hard. The hurricane season is now past, commencing in November and terminating in May. The last very severe "knock-down" wind, as the natives call it, occurred about two years ago, and did very serious injury to all the islands of the Samoan group. Barometer to-day 29° 59′; temperature of sea-water, 80°.

*7th June.*—A light north-west zephyr just dimples the intensely blue ocean; and although it is so smooth, no medusæ, not even a young Portuguese man-of-war (*Physalis urticus*) is to be seen.

*8th June.*—We hoped to have been at the mission church to-day at Manuatele, the principal island of the Manu'a group, the most easterly of the Samoan islands; but the wind, which has gone round the compass since yesterday, scarcely fills the sails. So "church was rigged" on board, as usual, a nautical order which sounds rather strange at first to a landsman.

At 10.30 this morning off Tau, the principal settlement of Manu'a; the picturesque islands of Ofu and Olosenga lie immediately opposite at about five miles' distance; they are evidently portions of a large crater. All the groups of the Samoan or Navigator's islands are of volcanic origin, with fringing coal reefs, for the most part encircling their shores.

One or two outrigger canoes of rather rough construction came off to us, not carved like those of the Savage Islanders, and their crews, being in a sort of half-European costume, did not appear to advantage. An old English coat over a Dracæna Titi looks rather an eccentric arrangement. The

Captain, several of the officers, and I went off in the pinnace, with a large quantity of photographic apparatus, and provision for the party, the ship standing out to sea for the night. We found the surf too high to attempt landing at Tau, so we went round to the neighbouring settlement at Faleasau, where, after a hard four-hours' pull in a tumbling sea, the wind having now come to blow fresh, we anchored in the little bay.

The natives landed us in their canoes, and received us with the kind hospitality for which the Samoan people are so noted. After the customary hand-shaking with the welcoming crowd, we were conducted to the Fala-tele or guest-house. Tui Faleasau, the principal man of the village, came in presently from behind a screen of siapo or native cloth. We were, of course, mutually polite; but, having no interpreter, our conversation was rather limited. Poor man! he was a sad object, his face being much distorted from paralysis, and his right hand was in so dreadful a state, that I wished etiquette had permitted his offering us his left. Amongst the crowd we observed many suffering from ophthalmia. Elephantiasis also seemed very prevalent.

We found that there was no English missionary

here at present, the only European on the island being a French lad, left sick by a trading-vessel two months ago. He had picked up a little of the language, and was useful to us, in explaining our wishes regarding our arrangements, some of which, no doubt, appeared singular enough; and, when they saw the tent pitched, and the little black one for photography with the cameras, and the other odd-looking apparatus, our hosts must have been somewhat puzzled by our mysterious proceedings. They, however, did all in their power to assist, carried our goods in their canoes carefully through the surf ashore, and brought them up from the beach.

We took up our quarters with a family whose house seemed the best in the village, to the evident chagrin of many applicants for our company. In the evening, as we sat in the Turkish fashion, and according to Samoan usage, cross-legged on clean mats at dinner, our proceedings were closely inspected by a large but well-behaved crowd, sitting round outside, who seemed to consider our beer and claret very good inventions, whilst we equally approved of their fresh cocoa-nut milk and delicious roasted bread-fruit. Our arrangements will be more easily understood by a description of our domicile, which will serve for all Samoan houses, as the plan adopted by the first chief who ceased to be satisfied with being "housed by the heavens," is, as they report, universally adhered to. Upon a raised platform of rough stones, covered with gravel, varying in diameter according to the size of the building, beyond which it extends from ten to twenty feet, stands what at a distance looks like a huge mushroom, the usual size being about a hundred feet in circumference. It is in fact a great dome-shaped roof, raised from the ground upon posts, about four feet high, and the same distance apart, between which a sort of blind, made of plaited cocoa-nut leaves, is let fall at night, or in stormy weather. This roof is so constructed, that it can be removed in three or four parts, and is sometimes taken by sea on a raft of canoes. It is supported in the centre by three posts, about twenty-five feet high. Rounded beams, cut from the heart of the breadfruit tree, which treated thus is very durable, are placed at equal distances horizontally, and tied firmly and very neatly with sinnet to the cross-pieces. To these are lashed closely a great number of small battens, also of the hard part of the breadfruit tree, in rows of six, generally of darker and lighter shades alternately. To this the thatch is made fast in a very ingenious manner; it is made of the long leaves of the sugar-cane, pinned like a fringe to reeds with the rib of the cocoa-nut leaf. This part of the work is done by women; and one, if she works hard, can prepare about fifty of these reeds in a day. Each is about five feet long, and in the way they are laid on, about four thousand are required for the roof of a good-sized house. The effect inside of these numerous reeds of the same size, carefully lashed with cocoa-nut cord, is very pleasing. The floor, of fine gravel, is covered with mats, clean ones being always laid for strangers. A house contains but one apartment, but bedrooms are formed at night by the mosquito tents, which are about eight feet long and five wide, made of dark siapo, and are let down at equal distances round the central post. On either side of it is a fireplace, a circular hollow, ten or twelve feet in diameter, lined with clay. House-building is a distinct trade, and the carpenter generally is well paid. No contract is entered into, but it would be a great disgrace to a man to have it said, "Oh, he paid his carpenter miserably; he is a contemptible fellow."[1] Our host, whatever price he paid, had

[1] So far as the individual himself is concerned, he suffers no more from the reproach than the rest of his tribe, for, in consequence of the sort of community of goods which exists amongst members of the same

managed to have a very well built roof over his head; and the supply of clean mats given to us was most bountiful.

After dinner, the people seemed much amused by watching us play at whist and backgammon. Our amusements were suddenly suspended by hearing the master of the house commence singing the evening hymn, in which most of the assembly, taking their books out of their waist-cloths, joined; and we, removing our hats also, added our voices to the best of our ability, hymn-books being handed to us. The psalm finished, our host made a long extempore prayer; the Lord's prayer concluding the service.

It certainly was a striking scene, half a dozen unarmed Englishmen sitting here in the midst of a crowd of half-naked islanders, and receiving a lesson of this kind from people so lately designated "ferocious savages."

As night drew on, more fresh mats were unrolled for us, and the family and ourselves gradually were all stretched in our appointed places. They wished us to use the mosquito tents, but as there was no humming heard, we preferred lying down in our clothes, with plenty of fresh air, notwithstanding

family or tribe, a man wishing to build a house or a boat has only to go round and ask for contributions.

their warning that we should be sorry for it before morning. About midnight, however, being made well aware of the hostile intentions of the advancing foes, we were glad to be shut in.

Looking out into the bright moonlight of the tropics, the feathery fronds of the cocoa-nut trees glistened in the rays against the dark hill side, which rose perpendicularly above the village; and the flying-foxes flitted, ghost like, over the dark foliage of the bread-fruit trees, from amidst the branches of which issued the sweet notes of a species of nightingale. Close to my head, there was a row of little Kannaka children, in nature's garb, each with its head resting upon a thick bamboo, laid between two trestles, the universal pillow in Samoa.

Rising at dawn, a few cocoa-nut shells full of water were with difficulty obtained. The supply at Faleasau is not very good, either in quantity or quality; indeed, that afforded by the cocoa-nut tree is more refreshing. Without this beautiful tree the islanders of the Pacific would be poor indeed;—food, drink, clothing, fishing, nets and lines, utensils, etc., are all provided by it, and nearly £30,000 worth of goods are brought now to Samoa annually in exchange for the oil produced from the nuts.

Until mid-day, we were busy with photography,

the operations exciting the liveliest interest; and having succeeded in obtaining one or two good pictures of the rich scenery around us, they seemed utterly bewildered on their being shown to them. The day was oppressively hot, and the ground was wet and steaming from the heavy showers during the night. We walked afterwards over the hill to Tau, and were glad sometimes to receive the assistance of the attendant crowd (of boys and girls chiefly) on the steep and slippery path.

Having first paid our respects to Tui Manu'a (King of Manu'a), a quiet gentlemanly old man, who received us very politely, although we could see that he was disappointed that we had not fixed our quarters here, where we found good entertainment had been provided for us. We accompanied Tauga, the resident superintendent of teachers, a Rarotongan, to his house. His smiling, stout, motherly-looking wife had a good lunch prepared for us, at the chief's cost. Pleasant-faced damsels fanned us as we partook of her baked fowls and yams, bread-fruit and palu-sammy, an excellent dish made of the tops of the Taro (the *Arum esculentum*), and cocoa-nut. We found it a great comfort to be relieved for a time from the incessant labour of driving away the hosts of flies, which here, as in

Egypt, one sees settled in numbers on the children's eyes, who seem to think it too much trouble to fight with them.

After a short rest, during which a rather unsatisfactory attempt at conversation was made, our host Tauga knowing but little English, we bade them adieu, promising to return and avail ourselves of their own and Tui Manu'a's hospitality, should we not go off to the ship. We returned, attended by a large company, to Faleasau, by the path which the chief had evidently caused to be weeded and swept for us yesterday. In places it is steep, and to-day as slippery as glass, and overhung throughout by the richest tropical vegetation. We left the shore at sunset in the cutter, the pinnace having gone before, and after a hard pull in the dark, got on board, just as the ship was bearing away from us, as we had not been seen in consequence of the heavy rolling sea. We had reason to think ourselves very fortunate in having done so, for in ten minutes afterwards it came on to rain in torrents, and to blow hard; not at all a pleasant night to spend in an open boat in the so-called Pacific.

11*th June.*—One native came off with us last night, as we had arranged to stand in again in the morning to settle our bills. He repented his adventure, no doubt, heartily, as he was wretchedly sea-sick as soon as he got on board the ship, as all natives accustomed only to canoes invariably are. This morning, notwithstanding the weather being very wet and squally, the natives came off in considerable numbers in large canoes, carrying thirty men each, and amongst them Tauga, the missionary, who breakfasted with Captain Cator and myself. His manners were very good, and there was something about him which commanded respect. He seemed to take much interest in the ship and the machinery, never having seen a steam-engine before. His companions generally were bent upon trading; some, we fear, made bad bargains, as it was found afterwards that one of the crew had been silvering pennies, which they preferred to dollars, it was said, seeing them transformed before their eyes.

## CHAPTER IV.

### PASSAGE TO TUTUILA.

LEAVING Manu'a at eleven o'clock, we stood over to Tutuila, and, favoured by a strong south-east wind, were under its bold coast before sunset. The mountains are from 2500 to 3500 feet in height, and their outline is highly picturesque.

12*th June*.—After a very disagreeable night, during which the rain came down in torrents, with heavy gusts of wind, we gladly breathed the fresh morning air, as it cleared up ; and we ran into the romantic harbour of Pago Pago. We saw the native pilot-boat standing toward us, from the little island of Annua seven miles to the north, but his services were not required by Mr. Libby the able master of the "Fawn." The harbour, which is an ancient crater, is very deep, but is completely land-locked by lofty mountains, under the protection of which a vessel with proper precautions might ride out even one of the fearful hurricanes sometimes experienced here between the months of November and May, which, as the natives say, *skin the land.*

To those who have never beheld tropical scenery, it is difficult to give any description which will enable them to realize the singular beauty of these islands. Here high rugged mountains, clothed with dense green forests, sink sheer down to the water; a grey precipice now and then relieving the eye. Against the blue sky the outline is broken by a graceful palm, or some high pinnacle, or by the waving bamboo or banana. Silvery sands stretch along in front of the narrow plain, shaded by thick groves of cocoa-nut trees, whose leaves wave and dance, reflecting the rays of the bright sun, underneath which are the scattered villages of the natives. Upon the narrow fringing coral reef, the dark green waves break dazzlingly, while at the head of the bay, the white cottage and mission church give an air of quiet civilisation to the scene, enlivened by numbers of canoes with their picturesque occupants moving about in all directions. Around H.M.S. "Fawn," lying at anchor in the glassy lake-like waters, a tiny fleet is crowded, and over all the deep blue heaven is shaded ever and anon by rolling clouds, borne in by the trade-wind, which *is seen* not felt.

Only one or two canoes came alongside when we first anchored, in consequence, we found afterwards, of an order given by the chief when the ship was sighted, that his people should not go off until it was known who we were. He thought it might possibly be one of the "Popy's" vessels, meaning the French, who might be coming to pursue, if possible, the same course they have taken in Tahiti, which has much alarmed the Samoans; and, as the Roman Catholic missionaries are chiefly Frenchmen, it is easy to understand how they have got the idea. It is greatly to be regretted that the different Christian churches should not be able to come to a definite arrangement regarding the distribution of their representatives in the islands of the Pacific, and that the different sects of Protestants and the Roman Catholics should clash in any way, as it is only a necessary consequence that at times, the missionaries meet with the reply, when urging their creed upon the aborigines, "Settle among yourselves which is the right religion, and then we shall know what to do." I landed in the afternoon with the Commander, and called upon the resident missionary, the Rev. Mr. Powell, a most excellent man, who evidently has the good of the people, amongst whom he has resided for seventeen years, really at heart.

We called also upon the chief Mauga,[1] who, being of the "blue blood," was sent for from Manu'a to Pago Pago at the death of the last Mauga—the chieftain of a Samoan tribe always bearing the same name. We found him sitting in his house, without any appearance of superior wealth or power; but there was that in his bold and dignified bearing which bespoke the chief whose word here still is law in most things. His wife, rather a tall, comely woman, was beside him; she did not wear when at home the tiputa, but was habited like her lord in Kannaka fashion; both wearing lava-lavas from the waist only, of coloured siapo; "perhaps all for heat was laid aside her wimple."

Mauga has always professed Christianity, and been on friendly terms with the missionaries, and followed their wishes; but his honour compelled him to call upon his people about three years ago to go to war, much to their disappointment and distress; as, notwithstanding all the arguments Mr. Powell could urge, having once done so, they thought it a necessary consequence that they must return to polygamy, night dances, and other heathen customs.

[1] Pronounced Maunga; the *g* in Samoan having always the nasal sound; the *n* is dispensed with in the missionary spelling, which I adopt.

PAGE 43.

Fr. a Photog. by Comdr R. P. Cator R. N

W. & A. K. Johnston Edinr

CHIEFS IN WAR COSTUME

Edmonston & Douglas

In the last engagement, a few weeks ago, having obtained a victory, and killed a number of the adverse tribe, it is to be expected they will be satisfied with the atonement now obtained for the death of the man whose murder was the original cause of the hostilities. This is the more likely to be the case, as war has not the same attraction now that fire-arms have been introduced, as in the old days, when the use of the spear and clubs gave more opportunity for the display of personal prowess in hand-to-hand encounters. Were it not for this, I believe all the efforts of the missionaries would avail little in putting a stop to this love of indulging, like the Highlanders of former days, in the excitement and glory of war, which provided them with subjects for song and story, and enabled the conquering chieftain to claim more than the regard given to the magistrate and lawgiver of peaceful times. And one can scarcely feel surprised at it, on seeing one of these splendid-looking men arrayed in the barbaric splendour of their war-costumes.

We saw to-day a large number of the Tutuilans, and I will venture to say, that in no part of the world could so many stalwart, handsome men be found amongst a similar number of people. The usual dress is the titi or kilt of the green leaves of the *Dracæna terminalis*, or a flowing lava-lava of coloured siapo, and sometimes of white cotton. The men are generally elaborately tatooed from the waist to the knees, in a most artistic manner. In their estimation, this supplied the place of dress; and even in ours it does so, having, with the narrow apron of dracæna leaves, the appearance of a pair of tight breeches. Indeed, so perfect is the deception, that in the account of a visit to the islands in 1772, the people are described as "being clothed from the waist downwards with fringes and long hose, made of a kind of silken stuff artificially wrought."

The women are nice-looking, and have good strong figures, but cannot generally be called pretty. Their dress is becoming, consisting of the siapo robes, or short petticoats of dracæna. Wreaths of scarlet hibiscus flowers in the hair are much in fashion, the effect being especially agreeable when the hair, cut short and brushed back, is powdered with fine coral lime. This is used, amongst other reasons, for the purpose of turning the hair to a reddish purple hue, which is much admired. The tipputa (or tippet like that of the Cingalese women, but without sleeves) is not so commonly worn as we expected; perhaps the old fashions having been

tog by Commander R.P. Cator R.N.

W. & A.K. Johnston Edin.

SAMOAN GIRLS IN USUAL DRESS

Edmonston & Douglas

resumed by the men, the ladies have followed, or set the example.

The sex is treated with the greatest consideration in Samoa. We saw several women sitting quietly in their canoes, whilst their cavaliers swam alongside, towing them through the surf, not because they are at all less at home in the water than their husbands and brothers; as we saw this afternoon, when a large number of girls were alongside, who were as often swimming about, laughing and talking, for about half an hour at a time in the water, as sitting in their boats, which they are constantly upsetting.

Their lives are too valuable to be sacrificed on the death of their husbands, as is the case in some parts of Polynesia, where the chiefs are interred in the grave with their unfortunate strangled wives. When a man dies in Samoa, his widow is generally taken by his brother, according to the Jewish custom, or by some near relative. Children are affectionately treated, but not judiciously, and many die from the over-kindness of their parents, who can deny them nothing, and permit them to eat whatever they like, and as much as they please. On the whole, a happier race of people could not be found than the Samoans. A scowling or discontented face is seldom seen; want or poverty is unknown, and nature has showered upon their country her choicest gifts. They are very fond of amusements; the inhabitants of the various villages frequently pay each other visits, and on these occasions, the evenings are usually spent in singing and dancing.

There is to be an entertainment of this sort to-night, at a village almost opposite the ship; and we are invited to another to-morrow night, given to a party expected from Leone, a place distant about ten miles down the coast. On these excursions, outside the harbour, large canoes are used, which carry from forty to fifty people. They are from thirty to sixty feet long; the keel is of one piece, and the sides are built up, not with long planks, but with pieces of wood, of irregular sizes and shapes, split out and smoothed with the hatchet, and most ingeniously stitched together with cocoa-nut sinnet, the lashings being passed through a rim left on the inner edge of each board. The canoe is made perfectly water tight with the gum obtained from the bread-fruit tree; and with such extreme nicety are the joints fitted, that on the outside, where the sewing is not visible, it is scarcely possible to detect them, without very close inspection. Along the bow and stern is generally a row of white shells

(*Cypræa ovula*), and some have a raised prow thickly studded over with these shells, and above, the figure of some bird or beast, the armorial bearing of the village to which the canoe belongs. De Bougainville gave these islands the appellation of L'Archipel des Navigateurs, from the constant use made by these people of their canoes; but the name is scarcely so applicable to them as to Tonga, and other groups, whose inhabitants are much more daring voyagers than the Samoans. The common canoes in daily use are merely hollowed logs, with rough outriggers, in the management of which the natives are very skilful, from constant practice, boys and girls paddling about in little dingies of similar construction from earliest childhood.

13*th June.*—The weather to-day is still very different from what we anticipated here at this season. Heavy showers again fell during the night, dense clouds veil the mountain tops, and the atmosphere is very hot and oppressive. Mr. Hunkin, formerly missionary at Manu'a, but now consular agent for Tutuila, came to-day from Leone, bringing with him his son and daughter, both interesting, good-looking young Samoans, much liker their mother's race than their father's, as we have observed to be the case with all the half-castes here. In their dress, manners, and feelings, they are thoroughly Kanakas, and preferred evidently to speak their native tongue. Perhaps their father has judged wisely for their happiness, for few of the possessors of all the good things civilized England can give are half so happy and contented as the Samoans.

In the evening we went to the dance. I believe all are not conducted so decorously as this was; were they so, it would be much better that the national amusement should not be discontinued, seeing that we give the light-hearted people no substitute in the way of pleasure. The company ranged themselves round the circle of the Fala-tele, and outside were many on-lookers. A bright fire was kept up with the dry leaves of the cocoa-nut, and dances in succession were performed first on one side of the house and then on the other, the light being shifted to the other fireplace. Places in the front row had been reserved for us, by the side of the chief dames of the village, and the propinquity to the performers was somewhat dangerous, when, in the excitement of the moment, they bounded and jumped, with shouts, apparently straight up over one's head. A low monotonous chant is kept up by the party on whose side the dancers enter, swelling always at the end of the line of the song, whilst they clap their hands loudly, and in the most perfect time, all together, to the sound of a small longa or native drum, the effect of which is pleasing.

Men and women generally dance separately, but sometimes together. On this occasion, first entered five or six splendid-looking fellows in full native costume, wearing small aprons of red dracæna, which, being oiled, glittered and reflected a dark red light. All the tatooing is visible, of course. On their heads were full wigs of a reddish colour, frizzed out gloriously, made of their own hair, which every man, for a certain period, allows to grow long, for the purpose of making these head-dresses, worn in war and in the dance.

Around their foreheads they twine strings of large beads, made from the pearl nautilus-shell, or coronets of the flowers of the scarlet hibiscus, which together look very handsome.

The performance cannot properly be termed dancing. They go through an infinite variety of strange motions and attitudes, springing up at times many feet from the ground, their agility and correctness being anxiously watched and criticised by the assembly,—especially the leader's, who is generally some young chief, whose every motion is instantly followed by all the others. In the rapidity and exactness of imitation and correct time consists the perfection of the performance.

When they left the house, a number of girls entered, who went through a somewhat similar set of evolutions, with infinite exactness and grace. It may seem incredible to our fair sisters in England that a young lady arrayed in no other garment but a mat tied round her waist should look handsomely dressed; but could they see these Samoan belles enter the circle in their full evening costume, with their coronets of nautilus-shell and scarlet hibiscus, and their necklaces of red and yellow flowers, I believe they would admit that their appearance is highly imposing. Some wore beautifully plaited fine mats, which are so highly prized that they cost more than a rich silk or satin dress. Others had white shaggy dresses, made from the inner fibres of the hibiscus, the amplitude of which would satisfy the most extensive patronesses of crinoline, and indulged in trains equalling in length those worn by the dames of England in former days, while their carriage and airs plainly showed that whatever we might think they felt themselves superior beings.

There was no ava-drinking to-night, everything being orderly and quietly conducted. The "Papalangis" contributed their share to the evening's amusement by a display of fireworks, with which the people were much delighted, as also with a hornpipe danced in the moonlight under a bread-fruit tree by the boat's crew.

Harbour of Pago-Pago.

Having landed the photographic tent and apparatus at a point down the bay, Captain Cator and I spent the forenoon there, taking views of the beautiful scenery and likenesses of the natives, as they stopped to witness the operations, which, as usual, excited great interest, every one seeming desirous to stand or squat in any position, provided his or her likeness were taken. As an instance of the good manners and obliging disposition of the people, when a canoe happened to intercept our view by passing, it was immediately stopped by its occupants, on our making a sign, though in one or two cases at considerable inconvenience to themselves, as the tide was rapidly falling on the reef.

Sailing over these coral reefs when the sky is clear and the water smooth is most interesting. Looking down into the depths, the various zoophytes resemble beautiful flowers of varied and brilliant colours; some large ones of delicate lilac, are exactly like bunches of thyme; but their beauty, of course, fades immediately on being exposed to the air, and the odour soon becomes most offensive. In and out among the branches glide and dart most brilliant coloured fish,—some of silvery whiteness, others bright blue,—sporting in these quiet depths, which one might well fancy the Peri's paradise of the Arab minstrel, who had gazed on similar beautiful scenes on the Red Sea shores.

## CHAPTER V.

### PAGO-PAGO.

On the 15th June we went to the mission-church, and heard Mr. Powell perform service, in the Samoan language, to an attentive congregation. The psalms were sung to the oldest-fashioned tunes, with the long dreary drawl one hears in a Scotch country kirk. The men's voices seemed better and more harmonious than the women's, whose notes had rather a harsh and metallic sound. I confess it was rather difficult to preserve one's gravity. Wherever one's eyes turned, they were sure to rest upon something most astounding in the way of bonnets. Under a huge coal-scuttle of native manufacture, built upon the most exaggerated scale of the fashion prevailing when Europeans first came to these islands, you saw the happy, contented-looking face of a girl, looking as though she had been got up for a pantomime, who, in her native head-dress of a single flower, would have been much more becomingly arrayed. Perhaps beside her sat her mother, who, with spectacles on her nose, pored over her book with an equally astonishing work of art overshadowing her shrunken figure. The bonnet is considered the proper costume for Sunday; but the notion is a mistaken one, and the missionaries would do well to make their religious services as little sombre as possible, especially with a naturally gay and light-hearted people as the Samoans are. For the sake of others, the next time we visit our excellent friend Mr. Powell, I hope to find that he has induced his fair parishioners to substitute straw hats for these odious inventions, otherwise his Papalangi hearers will exclaim, with Pat,—

> "Oh, lave off the bonnet,
> Or else I lave on it
> The loss of my wandering sowl!"

It struck me certainly that there was an air of listless weariness about the professing Christians when engaged in service in the mission-church. After the first excitement of the new religion has passed away, the natives are apt to become apathetic and indifferent; and it is not to be wondered at that the more imposing ceremonies of the Roman Catholic Church, contrasted with the bare and cold service of the Congregationalists, gains for the former many proselytes.

Leaving all differences of opinion and creeds out of the question, one would regret to see the clergymen of the London and other Missions fail in reaping the full fruits of their intrepidity and zealous endeavours in consequence of their opposition to each other.

As a body, they are deserving of great admiration. Many have become martyrs in the cause; and instances of true heroism and personal bravery, equalling the knightly feats of the olden time, are many in number. When a man, alone and unnoticed by his countrymen, amongst hordes of cannibals, boldly risks his life in the cause of religion, he manifests a degree of courage worthy of all fame. But such fame these brave men cannot even hope to win, as there is seldom more known, when they fall victims to the superstitious and ferocious violence of the islanders, than that they were massacred; under what circumstances, does not transpire. We heard from Mr. Powell an anecdote of Tauga, the Rarotongan teacher at Manu'a, which will serve to show the dangers and trials that await those who make the first attempts to reclaim the heathen, and also what stamp of men are chosen as native teachers. He had been sent to the Isle of Pines, which, like the adjacent large country of New Caledonia and the New Hebrides, is inhabited by a fierce Papuan race. Some time after he had commenced his adventurous labours, a chief came down to the village where he had established himself, with 500 armed followers, for the express purpose of killing him. Advancing with savage shouts and yells to the door, he called out, "Where are you, you pig, you dog? Come out, for I have come to kill and eat you." Tauga stepped forward with a dignified, quiet smile, saying, "Allofa," that is, "my love to you." Three times the same answer was given by him to the louder and more ferocious abuse of the savage warrior and his men. Just as they seemed worked up into fury, and about to rush upon him and his band of friends, Tauga, with no sign of alarm in his manner, and meeting his enemy's glance with a steady eye, walked close up to the chief, and repeated his salutation, "Talofa,"—"my compassion to you," holding out his hand to him. To the intense astonishment and indignation of his people, the painted savage threw down his club, and said,—"What? not afraid! this man's God must be the great God, since he trusts so

REV. MR. POWELL AND NATIVE TEACHER.

in him." He then shook his hand, and went into his house, protecting him during the remainder of his stay.

The remuneration of these teachers from the Society is very trifling; but their wants are few, their only care being that they should be able to have a white shirt and trousers to preach in on Sundays. To strangers visiting these regions, and seeing—even in those islands where life is now safe—the hardships the missionaries have still to undergo from the climate, want of necessaries to which they have been accustomed, the difficulty of going from place to place, over rugged mountains covered with dense jungle, or in canoes exposed to the fierce sun and fever-producing miasmas, it certainly appears that these men ought to receive a higher remuneration for their labours. It is true they came out here "to preach the Bible to the heathen, and if they have been able to do so with success, they have had their reward." But missionaries have wives and children, who require clothes and food and some European luxuries, which become necessities in the torrid zone, especially in so trying a climate as that of Samoa.

After twenty years' hard labour, and a faithful service, £120 a year is a small salary to support a family upon,—especially as children must be sent to a cooler climate when they arrive at a certain age.

I heard no complaints from any one of the clergymen themselves on the subject; but even the most contented and self-denying seemed to think it hard that when they get leave to go home for a time, their salaries should be stopped from the time they leave until they arrive in London; when, after a fortnight to see their friends, they must be prepared to make themselves useful in any part of the British territories where their services are required.

Things are changing every day in these islands, and the salary which would have been ample some years ago is not so now, as the price of native productions as well as foreign has much increased.

The Samoans especially are very hospitable, and in this part of the world a man can travel about with more certainty than in his own country of being kindly welcomed by utter strangers. But it would not do for the missionaries to be dependent upon the charity of the people, who contribute very largely to the general funds of the Mission. The amount last year received in Samoa was no less than £1200. Even in Tutuila, during the late disturbances, when, in consequence of their returning to heathen customs, many were debarred from being church members, that is to say, from receiving the sacrament, such as Mauga and his people, they still paid their usual voluntary subscriptions. We saw them sitting in the back part of the church (except the chief, who had his small pew, the only one in the building); many with their hair long and frizzed in war fashion; and, as it was Sacrament Sunday, we had an opportunity of observing that the number of men who had remained steadfast, and wore short hair, was but very small. All the women who were church-members were conspicuous enough by their bonnets, whilst the gayer portion of the younger ones had their hair cut short, and were uncovered. Another highly creditable mark of the proper feeling of these people is, that, out of respect for Mr. Powell, they never on a single occasion have a night-dance either in the villages of Pago-Pago or Leone, where he has his principal residence and schools. But the Samoans are a nation of gentlemen, and amongst themselves their politeness and ceremonious observance of their rules of society are very remarkable. In one respect they carry it to excess, common people addressing each other as chiefs; and one is constantly inclined to exclaim with Richard, " Where do all these chiefs come from?" the difficulty being to find out who is not of noble blood.

One cannot but feel that they contrast most favourably with the generality of Europeans who come amongst them. They draw, however, the distinction between the man whom nature has made a gentleman, and the mere "clothes'-horse," and have a thorough contempt for the rude vulgarian, whose manners betray his character, however rich he may be.

In their "fonos" or public meetings the strictest attention is paid to precedency; and it would be an excess of ill-breeding unheard of amongst themselves, to walk across the circle round which the chiefs are seated. Sometimes a white man, looking upon himself as so far superior to the "savages," that he may infringe all their rules, marches carelessly with his pipe in his mouth in front of the speaker. The only remark they make is, "Oh, poor white pig, he knows no better." To a foreigner who behaves as a gentleman they show every respect; using, when addressing him, the language of ceremony as when speaking to a great native chief. This dialect, so far as it goes, differs as much from the Samoan in common use, as the old court French from the English of the present day; or the language em-

MAUGA.

ployed by the Natchez Indians and ancient Peruvians in conversing with their superiors did from the plebeian tongue, although not possessing the richness of these American idioms.

18*th June.*—Yesterday there was exercise with small arms on the beach. The Kannakas were much surprised at the distance to which the rifles carried. Several of them were indulged in a trial of their skill as marksmen, but were not very successful. In their own fights they march up towards each other from the opposing ranks, one by one, and fire at close quarters. To-day, Mauga the chief, his wife and two attendants, amongst others, his adopted son, Feau, a noble-looking fellow, came on board the "Fawn," to see a display of artillery on a larger scale. They seemed thoroughly to enjoy the roar of the guns, which echoed and re-echoed amongst the rugged mountains. When the boats were manned, and a sham-fight was concluded by the Captain successfully boarding and taking his own ship, their admiration and delight knew no bounds, though somewhat abated by the heavy showers which drenched us, as is usual every day. The rain was unheeded, however, by the Samoan ladies in their excitement, though their siapo garments and garlands of flowers are not much adapted for stormy weather. Mauga was suffering from a severe and sudden attack of that scourge of the country, the fever which ends in elephantiasis; but, though in much pain, he behaved himself on the deck, and afterwards in the cabin, with perfect amenity and good-humour; his indisposition not for a moment betraying him into any breach of etiquette.

As usual, instead of being arrayed like some of his brother chiefs in ill-fitting European pantaloons, and a coat with gilt buttons, he wore his customary costume of flowing siapo, gathered round him in folds like a Roman toga. Feau was in the full dress of a leader of the tribe in war; and his tall head-dress and lofty plumes of scarlet feathers from Fiji, made him look gigantic. As far as thews and sinews are concerned, we seemed generally an inferior race to our visitors.

We went to-night by invitation from Feau to a dance, at the same village, Faga-saa, and we certainly saw, that when the restraint of strangers' presence was removed, or lessened by better acquaintance, the startling customs are such as to make it evident that the missionaries have good reason for their endeavours to put a stop to these entertainments.

The good-humoured wife of the chief man of the

village was sitting next me, with two fine twin children in her lap, and every now and then her colossal husband returned from the excitement of his most energetic performances, to caress his piccaninnies. Their love for their children is carried to such an extent, that they gratify every wish they express. Mothers nurse them till they are often well grown ; and it is not uncommon to see a child five or six years of age pull its infant brother or sister away, and coax the mother to let it take its place for a little. Circumcision is practised at the age of eight years.

## CHAPTER VI.

### UPOLU—APIA.

19*th June.*—This morning we took Mauga's portrait, and that of his family, and the ship being now replenished with water, wood, and other necessaries, we left our friends at Pago-Pago, with a real feeling of regret; even the crowd alongside in boats seemed all in low spirits at our departure. There is much to like about these people. They are brave and manly, and, at the same time, gentle and winning in their manners. They are also very honest. During the eight days we have been here, the decks have been crowded for some hours every day by people, surrounded by articles of great value in their eyes; the ports have been always open, and from their canoes they could easily have hooked out many things without being observed, but not one single thing has been taken! Where would the like occur in Europe? We went to Mauga's house, before leaving, to say good-bye, and as we stepped into the boat, Feau

MARY.

stood forward, and addressing Captain Cator in a stately manner, bade us farewell in the following words:—"May sickness be far from you; if it please the Lord, may we meet again; however that may be, may all prosperity ever attend you all." Mr. Powell, who kindly interpreted generally on all formal occasions, came round in the "Fawn" to Leone, where we anchored in the evening, bringing with him the Leone girl, Mary, who had been left in his charge.

The surf was very high, and it was rather exciting going through it in her father's large boat, in which he came off for us; his fourteen athletic paddlers, all in native costume—a titi of dracæna leaves—seemed in their glory, as we flew in on the tops of the rollers, chanting a wild song, which Mary led, in a high and joyful voice, evidently glad to be out of the "big ship," and amongst her own people. The village is finer than Pago-Pago, the houses being larger, and kept in better order. Situated upon a level plain, covered with beautiful bread-fruit trees, it has a pleasing look of comfort and prosperity. The groves of cocoa-nuts are more extensive; and we saw large quantities of oil being prepared in canoes raised on trestles by the beach. The background, like that of Pago, is high forest-clad hills, and the scenery to the westward is particularly fine. We took tea with Mr. Powell's family, and afterwards Captain Cator and I spent an hour at the agent's, sitting upon mats on the floor, as usual, smoking our cigars, in which delectable occupation all the members of the family joined, the girls with fresh-made cigarettes. The eldest daughter, like her sister, was very interesting looking, and was seated by the side of a young native chief, to whom she is engaged.

I inquired of them about the habits of the Ou-ou, or great cocoa-nut-eating crab, common here, and found the reports previously received from the natives, corroborated. Mr. Darwin mentions that in the Seychelles, and elsewhere, there is a species which is in the habit of husking the nuts on the ground, and then tapping one of the eyes with its great claw to reach the kernel. Its congener here ascends the cocoa-trees, and having thrown the nuts down, husks them on the ground: this operation performed, again ascends with the nuts, which he throws down, generally breaking them at the first attempt, but if not successful, repeating it until the object is attained. Wherever one goes here, individuals of the crab genus are to be seen, well deserving the appellation of their great relative; for

Fr a Photog. by Commander R P. Cator R.N.

W & A K Johnston Edin^r

FEAU WIFE AND HENCHMAN.

Edmonston & Douglas

not content with robbing the occupants of different land and sea shells of their lives, they walk off with their houses, and are to be seen marching about in all directions with divers-shaped tenements on their backs, out of which the natives have an odd way of whistling them.

20*th June.*—Landed again this morning, and proceeded, in an even-down pour of rain (which kept us in durance of stifling hot air all night), to the Fala-tele, where the principal men of the place and neighbourhood were assembled. Their disappointment was great that Captain Cator could not comply with their request to go through the same exercise which had so delighted their neighbours, and of which some of their townsmen had been witnesses ; notwithstanding this, however, they agreed to consider the wish urgently expressed by him regarding the supply of water, etc., on more liberal terms than hitherto, to ships visiting the bay.

There is no chief here at present, the man whose birth entitles him to the position preferring to hold the office of Tu-la-fale, or "ruler of the lands;" master of the household, in fact, which confers upon the holder a great deal of power, and considerable pecuniary (*i.e.*, "fine mats") advantages. The addresses were, as usual, made by the orators, with fly-flappers, their distinguishing badge of office, over their shoulders.

As the rain continued all day in torrents, we were obliged to stay in Mr. Powell's house, when we had an opportunity of seeing his collections of plants indigenous to the islands, and other interesting curiosities, from which he liberally added to ours. We saw here good specimens of the native manufactures. The siapo, or common cloth, is made from the inner bark of the paper-mulberry; first scraped with shells, and then beaten out into a thin tissue with wooden mallets, the pieces being joined together with arrow-root paste. Some of the mats, plaited with strips of the leaves of a species of pandanus, are very beautifully made, and are handed down from generation to generation. "Englishmen like gold, Kannakas fine mats," they say, when you tempt them to sell one. The consul told me he had seen some old and tattered ones, in appearance utterly valueless, fetching, from the associations connected with the history of their former owners, 150, or 200 dollars. The currency in Samoa, from the trade at Apia being chiefly with American whaling ships, is in dollars and cents.

There is another particularly fine kind of mat, made from the inner bark of a species of hibiscus, from which they make "those" bonnets. Here at Leone we saw with pleasure that plain broad-brimmed hats of this pretty material were coming into fashion. The native spears and war-clubs are now not easily obtained, being also valued as heir-looms, as they have ceased to make them, since, like the New Zealanders, they have taken to the deadlier musket.

We were off again in the evening, and ran across to Upolu, distant from Tutuila about sixty miles. This fine island, considered one of the richest and most beautiful in the Pacific, is about 140 miles in circumference, and has a population of 16,000 or thereabouts; that of Tutuila being under 5000.

21*st.*—The morning was dark and rainy; and it was late in the afternoon before we could see the mountains and bold coast sufficiently, to run into the harbour of Apia, which is formed by coral reefs extending from both headlands of the narrow bay. As we approached it, the vessels at anchor appeared to be moored along the shore, without any shelter whatever.

We had expected to have beautiful weather in these parts, the rainy season being now far past. But it seems that during the last five years, as in Australia, there has been much more bad weather than was ever experienced before, so far as the natives remember, and an excessive amount of rain has fallen—the trade-winds becoming more and more uncertain. Most probably the immense quantity of ice seen of late years far north has much affected the climate of the Pacific. We found Apia quite a civilized-looking place; three large whaling ships were lying at anchor, and several smaller craft. Numbers of European-looking edifices, ugly and matter-of-fact affairs, with iron roofs, fronted the bay, and over two of the largest floated the flags of the English and Hamburgh consuls. Alas for the Kannakas! their interesting simplicity has been much worn off here, by their association with their new neighbours.

There are some two hundred Europeans settled here, many of them no credit to the country they claim to belong to. Our consul is son of the missionary *par excellence*, Mr. Williams, whose melancholy fate is well known. He is well fitted for the office: having been born in one of the islands, and passed most of his life amongst the Polynesians, he has the great advantage of being thoroughly conversant with their manners, customs, and language; and the interests of the Samoans will be protected whilst he holds the office. Although his sympathies are in

Fr. a Photog. by Commander R.P. Cator R.N. W. & A.K. Johnston, Edinr.

SCENE IN APIA BAY

Edmonston & Douglas

their favour, he does not seem inclined to pass over their misdeeds; and we found that he had a considerable number of complaints against them, chiefly for failing in completing the payment of fines inflicted for misdemeanours, by persons in various parts of the group, which will entail a much longer stay in Samoa than Captain Cator had intended.

The principal trading-establishment here is that of Mr. Unselm, the Hamburgh consul, who exported from Apia last year nearly seven hundred tons of cocoa-nut oil. He has a number of small vessels trading to the different islands to the north for pearl, and tortoise-shell, and oil; and is adopting a system which will be beneficial in many ways to others as well as himself, of planting cocoa-nut trees on all the desert cays and islands.

We found the people here all in a state of anxiety, in consequence of the threatened invasion of King George of Tonga, who is expected to arrive every day with a large armed force. He is a formidable enemy, being in possession of two brigs, and, it is said, a hundred double-canoes, capable of carrying from sixty to a hundred men each. He comes ostensibly to demand satisfaction for the death of a Tongan, murdered some time ago at Savaii. If the murderer is given up, his visit will be a friendly one; but no doubt he hopes that excuse may be afforded him for endeavouring to re-establish the ancient sovereignty of Tonga over its own parent state Samoa.

The fact is, George himself being partly a usurper of the throne of Tonga, requires constantly to make war with his neighbours, to keep his turbulent chiefs from mischief at home.

The distance from Samoa to Tongataboo is 500 miles, but the Tongans exercised feudal rights formerly over Wallis' Island or Uea and Fotuna, several hundred miles farther. The difference of a few degrees of climate much affects the energy of the inhabitants of the different groups. The Tongans, the Rarotongans, and Niuans, are all much more active than the Samoans, to whom nature has been so bountiful, that there is little necessity for any exertion on their part in providing themselves with food.

22*d June.*—Rainy, hot, and oppressive. This day we went to the Bethel Church, where certainly we listened to a most unprofitable service. There being no one bold enough to raise the tune, the minister apologized and read the hymns, and then preached a sermon, which was simply a tirade against the "poor Pope," as he called him, and the Catholic missionaries on the island, for withholding the Bible from the natives, geologists also receiving their share of the anathemas, being in some mysterious way chargeable with the same offence. One regrets much to see how religious differences influence the missionaries of different sects. With regard to the Catholic priests, it might have been supposed that a fellow-feeling of admiration would have induced their opponents to draw a veil over their errors, and that the consideration of a self-sacrificing zeal, equal to their own, would have inspired a more Christian sympathy for all who preach the Cross in the hearts of the sternest enemies to form and ceremony. But unfortunately the jealousies existing even between the Wesleyans and the clergymen of the London mission, are equally detrimental to the interests of both.

The Roman Catholic priests live as frugally as any other missionaries, and the spirit which animates them generally, may be safely believed to be that expressed by an old and respected priest living in the interior of Fiji, who, when remonstrated with for not trying to obtain more of the luxuries and even necessaries of life, said to the Consul, "The greater the reward hereafter."

I accidentally heard to-day of the existence of an

almost wingless bird in these islands, called by the natives Manu-ma-a (not Manu-ma, which is the resplendent cock-bird of a species of dove). Mr. Williams had one of these birds alive for some time, twenty years ago, and afterwards sent the skin home, but it was lost; and the cats, which are now wild in great numbers in the mountains, have almost extirpated them, so that the natives, although offered a large sum for a specimen, gave small hopes of being able to obtain one. From the description, it must resemble in shape the Notornis of New Zealand, as, when I made a rough sketch of that rare bird, the natives to whom I showed it immediately said, Manu-ma-a. It is also nocturnal, and possesses a handsome plumage of a dark colour and iridescent, they say, which however I should doubt, as being contrary to the distinguishing plumage of the class to which I presume it belongs. The Maories, however, describe that of the Moa to have been a dark purple, changing to blue or black. Like the Weki and Kiwi or Apteryx, it is very inquisitive, and used to be caught by the natives when it came peering about to examine the cause of any strange noise. It can take long hops or jumps with its short wings outspread, and is in the habit of flapping them repeatedly as it perches on the lower branches of trees. It is another curious instance of an almost wingless bird, of peculiar appearance, being found in an island remote from any mainland, and will soon probably also have disappeared, like the Dodo, leaving nothing known of it but its name.

23*d June.*—Siu Manutafa, chief of Apia, his son, and another young man, came on board to-day, all in European costume. The elder chief being a man of good presence and easy self-possessed manners, did not look so uncomfortable in his unwonted garb as the others in their blue coats and gilt buttons. In the course of conversation, which the Consul interpreted, Captain Cator expressed his regret that the chiefs did not join in putting a stop to these petty outrages, and to the delay in payment of fines and debts to traders, which are injurious to the character of his countrymen, which otherwise stands high; explaining to him that one great cause of the power and prestige of the English name throughout the world is the maintenance of public and private faith. He fully acknowledged the truth of his remarks, but said the government of their country being of so democratic a form, any interference on the part of one chief with the affairs of his neighbours, would be regarded as impertinent, and be resisted by the people. There is certainly much need for some change in Samoa; and it would be well if any able man of the Malietoa, the principal family, should be able to establish his power over the whole group.

On the death of the old Malietoa, who was a very powerful chieftain, his daughter Emma was on the point of being chosen the Malietoa; but in consequence of the opposition of one of her own family, the power was placed in the hands of the brother and son conjointly, and Emma, a quiet retiring woman, gladly remained in her private station, though recognised as lady of highest rank among the Samoans.

The present holder of the honours is not popular, nor has he the means of taking up the various chiefdoms, which would require a large outlay of fine mats, large presents being expected by the different subordinate chiefs from the receiver of the title of Tui Atua, etc. This will be more easily understood when it is known that a chief may on his deathbed, or during his life at any time, nominate as his successor any one of his family. But it does not follow that afterwards the people will abide by his nomination; and if the adopted heir, son or nephew, is unpopular, they frequently refuse to

Fr. a Photog. by Commander R. P. Cator R.N.

W. & A. K. Johnston Edin.r

EMMA MALIETOA AND ATTENDANT.

Edmonston & Douglas

recognise him, and select some other person of the same blood more generally liked, who is confirmed as Malietoa, Mauga, Tui-manua, or whatever the family title may be. Although the head of the race, who bears the titular distinction, holds the lands of his father as his own, and has the right of disposing of a portion of it, should he venture to break the entail, as it were, and do so without being duly authorized by all the members of the family, publicly assembled, they would at once deprive him of his position, and confer it upon another. "Uneasy lies the head that wears a crown" in Samoa, as elsewhere. There is great jealousy existing amongst the principal chiefs, and they never go to sleep without guards on the watch, lest they should be murdered by the often unbidden retainers of some rival chief. They come in the darkness of night, oiled all over, and with their hair cut short, so that they cannot be easily laid hold of, and like the Thugs, gently tickle the sleeping unfortunate until he is in the position required for effecting his destruction in a manner similar to that by which Edward II. perished. The instrument used is the slender barbed "sting" of the Ray, which, penetrating further and further into the intestines, causes a certain but cruelly lingering death.

This jealousy stands greatly in the way of permanent improvements being effected. There are no roads in Samoa, as in Niue, Rarotonga, and other places, where there is one powerful chief, or a patriarchal form of government. The present political state of these islands is the one of all others most likely to cause retrogression in civilisation. The war which commenced in 1848, and lasted nine years, arose from the insolent exactions of the "Malo" (which word expresses the power of the conqueror),—a sort of feudal right exercised by the dominant confederation of chiefs, whose headquarters were at the small island of Manono, and whose influence depended chiefly upon their possession of the strong natural fortress of Apolima. It resulted in the abolition of that power, and the general independence of the several petty states or communities. Some of these are now under the government of a chief or king, as Tui Atua, whilst others cannot settle who is to be their ruler. Each of the communities has its own laws and customs, uniting in districts of six or more, for offensive or defensive purposes. It is all very well when the chiefs or the heads of powerful families are lovers of order. In some villages where such a happy state of things exists, all is well arranged, and there is an appearance of prosperity, as at Leone, etc. In others, the squalor and disorder attest the evil influence of a dissipated or turbulent chief. The people are well aware themselves of the desirability of having a general code of laws throughout the island, and a sort of federal government; and it is to be hoped that the efforts of the Consul, the missionaries, and the Captains of Her Majesty's vessels of war may be successful. It will be fortunate if an influence of this kind can be brought to bear now, as affairs are evidently in that state of anarchy and confusion which has resulted in the lamentable condition of New Caledonia and the New Hebrides, where the hands of the inhabitants are against their neighbours, and the comparatively good order which has prevailed under the powerful Malietoas, the Tu Puas, and others, is likely to be overturned.

It is the recognition of the power of the chief which has made Tonga formidable to its neighbours and well ordered at home. Perhaps it may be well if King George should attempt to fulfil his intentions; it may possibly result in bringing the internal affairs of Upolu and Savaii into a more wholesome condition, as the chiefs will be inclined to unite together in resisting him.

Siu Manutafa preferred a request that the gunner of the "Fawn" might be allowed, to-morrow, to give his soldiers some instructions in drill, which the Captain has granted him. Though barbarous customs still remain in full force, in many respects the chiefs are civilized in their habits, and most persons of position amongst the natives can read and write in Samoa, which is ripe now for taking an onward step, as the Sandwich Islands have done. If the opportunity be lost now, it may be gone for ever.

View at Apia.

# CHAPTER VII.

## UPOLU.

*24th June.*—The company of soldiers was paraded to-day in front of the Consulate. They marched into the village with a drummer in front, and officers, the chiefs' sons, walking alongside, in blue swallow-tailed coats and gilt buttons, with swords in their hands, fashioned in divers countries and in divers shapes. The men were in quaint uniforms, rather trying to the risible organs, consisting of coatees cut from scarlet regatta-shirts, braided with black and ornamented with a profusion of buttons, white trousers, shoes for the nonce, and red caps, in which each wore such ornaments as pleased him. One young fellow of about six feet two, evidently considered a large Birmingham brooch, with imitation cairngorm, a "stunning" affair. They were all armed with muskets and bayonets of American manufacture, and went through their drill very creditably, under the directions of their own serjeant. Mr. Pounds gave them some hints, as well as he could, under the difficulty of ignorance of their language. These they quickly availed themselves of, following the evolutions as shown them by the boat's crew, marching with them very readily, and requiring, evidently, but a little practice to be made an efficient corps. They were all fine strapping fellows, and in stature towered over the English sailors. I told the chief he ought to put them in lava-lavas and jackets, and he seemed more reconciled to the idea of giving up his motley uniform when he understood that our Highland soldiers were somewhat similarly attired. The Samoans, though idle and less energetic than some of the Polynesians, have always held the palm as warriors, being very brave and powerful men, and possessing much adroitness and quickness of sight. One chief has been known to defend himself against a host of enemies, turning aside their spears with the sword in his left hand, with extraordinary agility, whilst with his right he made good use of his war-club. Unfortunately, every man "fights for his own hand, as Harry Wynd did," discipline, even among such as the Tongans, being hitherto unknown; and now that the bullet brings death to the chief as well as his henchman, it tells against the leader, conspicuous by his towering plume, with double effect.

It is a mistake, however, to suppose that the introduction of the musket has been a misfortune to these people generally, so far as loss of life is concerned, for their engagements now are fewer and much less bloody than when they fought hand to hand, with their clubs and tomahawks.

*26th June.*—To-day the wind is blowing harder, and the weather is more disagreeably wet than ever. We have not had a fine day yet in Apia. The harbour looked quite gay this morning before the rain set in, there being five vessels besides the "Fawn." Among them the French despatch-boat, the "Latouche Treville," had come in from Tahiti by way of Penrhyn Island; it is said that her business is to look after King George's movements. This idea seems little relished by the Samoans, who say, "What have they to do with us? We have not asked for their assistance."

The commander dined with us on board the "Fawn" to-day. The only news we received from him was that, in consequence of a blight amongst the cocoa-nut trees, the unhappy natives of Penrhyn are starving, having no bread-fruit or taro there, and in consequence he is come to remove a number of them to Tahiti; the "Latouche Treville" having been despatched upon this humane mission instead of for the purpose of initiating any measures affecting the liberties of the people of Upolu.

Apia is a place of considerable resort for American whalers during the season. It is to be feared much evil has resulted from their visits to many islands of the Pacific. In numerous cases their lawless crews, men of all colours and nations, are under the command of timid and inexperienced masters, often themselves devoid either of principle or humanity. But there are many notable exceptions of course, and some of their captains are as much distinguished for proper feeling as for daring intrepidity.

We had the pleasure of meeting frequently, at Mr. Williams' and on board the "Fawn," Captain Grant of the "Jason," whose well-ordered ship bore witness to his seaman-like qualifications. For thirty-five years he has been in the habit of cruising in this part of the ocean, and no one has seen more, probably, of the various people who inhabit its thousand isles than he has, especially to the north of the Line,—the Carolines, the Ladrones, and Kingsmill group; together with isolated and interesting ones, such as Byron, Ocean, and others, densely peopled by attractive and comparatively inoffensive races. Regarding these, he gave me much curious information, which made me envy him, as his ship bore away for these imperfectly-known regions. The deeds which these men do, and the tales which they have to tell, are startling indeed, and some of the experiences of their hazardous occupation would scarcely be credited by those who have never heard before about the exciting but perilous chase of the sperm-whale.

Captain Grant said that on one occasion, when he was a young man, he had struck and made fast to a whale, a little before sunset. After running a short time, he saw the signal made from the ship to cut adrift and return. Excited with the sport, however, and also, no doubt, considering the dollars, he determined to hold on, if possible, particularly as the whale, contrary to the usual habit, was going before the wind, so that the ship would be able to keep near him. All night long the grand quarry towed the boat at the rate of eight or nine knots; at daylight he sounded, running out a thousand fathoms of line, and then rising to the surface, and seeing the boat, he darted furiously at it, and crushing it in his ponderous jaws, bit it into small fragments in his rage. The boats from the ship were now near, and picked up the men. He himself had jumped overboard with his lance, and swimming up to his giant adversary, now blind with fury, succeeded in inflicting the death-wound. This whale measured ninety feet in length, being one of the largest he ever saw killed. On another occasion, he was caught in the bight of a line as it ran out, and, before the men had time to cut it, he was carried far down into the ocean depths. When it slackened all seemed pitchy darkness, and he knew not which was above or under; but, striking out, he rose to the surface half dead, and was picked up almost insensible, close to the spot where he had gone down, so straight do the monsters dive. One of his legs bears the terrible marks left upon it when he was for some moments in a whale's mouth. A large bull having been struck, he turned and seized the boat in his jaws, and Grant's leg at the same time, which was nearly stripped to the bone.

Many may be inclined to think these stories "Yankee yarns," but there was a truthfulness about Captain Grant which left no doubt on the minds of those to whom he related some of the adventures of a long life in these regions, where his perils and escapes have been many. Amongst others, I may mention one, which might have ended, as such affairs have often done, in the loss of the ship and crew (as was the case in the same neighbourhood not many months ago), had it not been for the amusing consequences of the superstitious belief, so generally entertained by the Indians, that the spirits of their ancestors take up their abode in birds or beasts.

Off an island near the Line, some time ago, the natives came on board the ship in great numbers, and were thronging in over the bulwarks in a very suspicious manner, whilst more canoes were seen coming off from the shore with armed crews. They were consulting on board how they should get rid of their visitors without a collision, when one of the sailors happened to go near a large white cockatoo, who immediately raised his crest, and commenced his garrulous speech. Instantly, with the wildest exclamation of alarm, the savages jumped overboard as fast as they could, and, warning their friends of the presence of this awful "Aitu," they made for the shore; nor could any persuasion induce one to venture into his presence again.

Another vessel had a somewhat similar escape at Byron Island. The natives had come off, I was told, in the same way, in formidable numbers, and in large canoes. They boarded the ship, as she was going fast through the water, by throwing lines, with cocoa-nuts attached, into the rigging. The decks were crowded by a jabbering assembly, when the master, alarmed, went down into the cabin, and armed himself with cutlass and revolver; but, as he ascended the companion-ladder, found himself suddenly so completely squeezed up, that he could not make his way to the deck. Unwilling to commence hostilities with such odds against him, a thought struck him, and he called out to the cabin-boy to give them some music. No sooner had a barrel organ, which he happened to have, commenced playing "Awa, Whigs, awa," or some such ditty, than the horrified natives, panic-stricken, immediately fled from the angry god of the whale-catching white men.

The sperm-whale is gradually becoming scarcer in these seas, and more wary; the ferocity too of the bulls seems by all accounts to be increasing; the destruction of boats is of much more frequent occurrence. Like the Indians, they have much reason to fear the destruction of their race. Daily diminishing in numbers, they are driven into unwonted latitudes to seek their food, and safely to rear their young, for which they display great fondness.

The capture of the leviathan must be indeed a grand sight. The speed with which the sperm-whale rushes in its "flurry," as it is called, when its nearly exhausted energies are expended in one last effort to escape, is tremendous. The boat is dragged through the foaming sea at a rate that renders everything invisible to the crew, except foam and spray, and roaring waters mingled with blood, which the monster spouts high in air. But it is soon over, and turning with wrathful looks upon his puny adversaries, he rolls over on his mighty side, and dies.

The length of the whaling voyage is from four to five years, and they often run considerable risks in returning, from the leaky and decayed condition of the ship. One droll man facetiously informed us that he, Captain Fisch, "had been commander of a comical ship, through which the waves went, instead of she going through the waves, for two years, during which time he strained the waters of the Western Pacific three times!"

The profits of a successful cruise are large; and Captain Grant was soon about to return home with a fortune, I believe, of £30,000, which he well deserves. His only anxiety seemed to be the risk of losing all the fruits of his labour by the hands of privateers, or rather of pirates, on the coasts of the United States; more than one whaler having lately met this miserable fate when within a few days' sail of home, after years of privation.

## CHAPTER VIII.

### UPOLU—TUTUILA.

27*th June.*—We left Apia this afternoon in gloomy weather, to beat against the trade-wind back to Tutuila. The consul, Mr. Williams, came in the ship to make inquiries into an affair between his deputy, Mr. Hunkin, and one of the chiefs of that island, upon whose land a boat had been destroyed by a party during the war. They allege that this was done in consequence of the disregard of the Tabu which was over the particular part of the beach where they landed, because there had been lately buried there a great chief, and, according to their custom, the penalty was inevitable.

28*th June.*—The weather has been most disagreeable, hot and steamy. All night the rain poured down as it only does in these low latitudes. The wind, however, has favoured us, and we are this evening in sight of Tutuila, which we scarcely anticipated.

29*th June.*—After another miserable night, the rain being heavier and heavier, we have this morning a pleasant change.

A light north-west wind brings us fresh air, and we seem to breathe again. The sky is clear, and we saw this morning the island of Savaii in the distance, Upolu, and the whole of the outline of the sharp-peaked mountains of Tutuila, at the same time, which we have never done before. Calling off Leone, Mr. Hunkin came on board, and we steamed round in a calm to our old anchorage at Pago-Pago. The harbour to-day is as smooth as a mirror, and reflected in its calm depths the shadows of the beautiful hills, their shaggy woods, cliffs, and cocoa-nut palms. We called on Mauga, who gave every assistance to expedite the business. His advisers sat respectfully around whilst he talked with Mr. Williams. The chief with whom the matter is to be settled is Leato, the leader of the tribe with whom he had been fighting. According to suggestion, he immediately despatched a messenger with a letter, promising perfect safety to him and his people whilst here, if he would come and have the inquiry held on board the "Fawn." It remains to be seen whether pride will not prevent his coming, even should he place sufficient confidence in Mauga's safe-conduct to return through his territory. The Pago-Pago people would evidently not feel much regret, if it be necessary to use force, should their late adversaries refuse to come and have the matter investigated.

All our friends here are delighted to see us again. They said they shed many tears when we went away,—an eastern hyperbole, I dare say. This being Sunday, no canoes were moving about, and few people were outside their houses. Soon after we sat down in Mr. Powell's cottage, the bells rang, and all the people who had come to welcome us hurried away to listen to the Samoan teacher, Mr. Powell being at Leone. This rigid observance of Sunday presents a rather humiliating contrast with its profanation in more favoured regions. Whatever their real feelings on the subject may be, the natives believe it to be an imperative duty to respect the day, great though the temptation may be to amuse themselves, as on this occasion; and they regard it so far as to refrain from attacking an enemy on Sunday, even under favourable circumstances. It may possibly be from superstitious fear of evil consequences; but from whatever motive they act, Sunday is most strictly kept, as much so as in Edinburgh, without the attendant miseries.

The Protestant missionaries have had their hands strengthened by a circumstance which occurred lately in the bay. A girl was being carried to the grave by her friends, having been, to all appearance, dead for some time, when suddenly she awoke from the trance in which she had been. When recovered a little, being asked what she had seen, she told her wondering friends that she had been at the gate of heaven, and was met there by an angel, whom she described with most imaginative minuteness, convincing all the superstitious people that she had actually seen all she related. She was told by this celestial being that there was but one religion only, and that the people who alone could gain admittance at the gate were Protestants. Many of the Roman Catholics here, it is said, have taken the alarm, and left their priest. We spent the evening on shore, at the mission-house, where a considerable number of people were assembled to hear all the news of the outer world from Mr. Williams. On being told of the arrival at Apia of the French ship, they expressed their doubts as to their intentions as strongly as their countrymen at Upolu.

Mr. Williams explained the code of laws he has drawn up, and which has been accepted by the Apia people. Most of the regulations were approved of, but some, although admitted to be very proper and good, especially those for the punishment of breaches of the seventh commandment, were, they said, very hard for Samoans to observe. For although by their own custom death is frequently the result of detection, and the murder of the seducer is not considered to be a crime, infidelity is very common. There is no doubt that even still the greatest license is taken by the men, especially young chiefs, who, although not exactly polygamists, as far as one can make out, marry many wives, putting away one to take another, chiefly for the sake of the dower of fine mats,—the "Tonga," as it is called. I saw one chief at Leone, a man of about forty-five years of age, who had been married, in Samoan fashion, fifty times. Their morality, it is very evident, is more nominal than real; and it is hardly possible that it should be otherwise, considering the kind of conversation to which children of tender years are accustomed to listen, and the way in which they live. The young women of good blood, however, seldom go astray before marriage, as the disgrace to their families is great if they do so.

30*th June*.—A message was received this afternoon, couched in polite language, from Leato, to the effect, that however desirous to show due respect by acceding to the request that he should come to Pago-Pago, it was impossible for him to do so until the "Fonotalaga," *the meeting to clear away the clouds,* had been held. This could not be, until Bull-a-ma-cow, otherwise the raging bull, a chief of Upolu, came to Tutuila, he having been chiefly instrumental in bringing about the war, in consequence of the alleged desecration of his mother's grave by the man who had been killed. The custom, prevailing throughout Samoa, of burying their friends close to their houses, that they may be always in sight, makes it rather difficult at times to avoid stepping accidentally upon the graves in some of the villages, which is a grave offence.

Leato, however, proposed to meet Captain Cator and the council at a village, immediately beyond the boundary of Mauga's land, which arrangement is accepted.

We spent a considerable part of the day in Mauga's house, where he prepared a feast for us, consisting of the usual delicacies, pig, fowl, taro, bread-fruit, and palu-sammy. The porker was roasted and served up whole, with his stomach filled with taro-tops and red-hot stones. We had seen him running for his life a short time before, and knocked over with a stone, affording within a couple of hours a little exciting sport, and then a dinner to the company. We had also to go through the ordeal of tasting the ava after seeing it prepared, the root being chewed on the occasion, fortunately, by two nice-looking girls. The taste and smell resemble rhubarb. The bowl is handed round, and presented with ceremonious politeness by a cup-bearer, often a fair damsel, who, standing at the greatest possible distance, makes a graceful inclination, and holding it at arm's length, presents it to the person whose name is called out by the master of ceremonies. The effect of this preparation, when drunk in large quantities, is not like that of alcohol, or fermented liquors, being rather that of a powerful narcotic, producing partial paralysis and torpor of the limbs. It is said to be valuable as a remedy for cutaneous affections.

1*st July*.—May-day in Pago-Pago—that is, the yearly festival which takes place in the principal villages, when the contributions towards the mission are collected—is celebrated to-day, having from various circumstances been delayed this year. Boats full of people had been coming in yesterday from the adjacent villages. It had been a melancholy day for pigs and fowls, which were being knocked over with stones and sticks in all directions by the villagers, on hospitable thoughts intent. The "*girls were weaving baskets*" from the leaves of the cocoa-nut, to hold the presents of food of various kinds, which the lads carried in procession to the chief, and others, wherewith to entertain the numerous visitors. Early this morning, the booming sound of the longa, or native drum, came across the water, and all was bustle and merriment when we landed. Old and young were engaged in arraying themselves in "all they had of rich;" and as the different groups marched in single file, with slow-measured tread, towards the church, they presented a very gay and interesting appearance.

The women and girls were in full siapo robes, and many wore fine mats one over another, and long trains sweeping the ground, with gay tiputas of blue and scarlet, and flowers in their hair. The men wore also large siapo lava-lavas, and imposing head-dresses. In the church, crowded to the doors, addresses were delivered by Mr. Powell first, after he had read out the names of the subscribers of oil, etc., then by the Consul and native teachers, and lastly by the Captain and myself. Mauga, who was dressed in his usual style, replied in a quiet, manly speech. He thanked us for the honour done to him and his people, by the presence of so many Papalangi chiefs. England and Samoa had to-day met together. He regretted that his people had not this year been able to give so much as he could wish, but the war had made them very poor, which, much as he regretted to see the consequences, it was impossible for him, consistently with his honour, to avoid.

Afterwards, a plate was handed round, and all put in their shillings or sixpences. It was worth while coming back to Pago-Pago to witness this very interesting scene. The Samoans are very fond of public speaking, and their style of oratory is eloquent and forcible. The great "talking-men" are most influential personages, and are the depositaries of the history of the chief families, and the traditional story of the country, handing it down from father to son with the most scrupulous care and secrecy. The old talking-man of the Malietoas died a short time ago; only a few days before his death, he communicated to his son all the legends of the past in his possession, and handed over to him the most ancient record in Samoa—the genealogical tree of that family, which would convey but little information to the uninitiated, being a tall stick with certain marks or signs, understood by those men only. In their speeches, allegory is much used, and it is often beautiful and touching ; and you may venture to speak very strongly, if a well-pointed fable is introduced, or entertaining legend, especially if you wind it up with a joke. Telling them anecdotes of some of Britain's greatest chiefs,—I ventured to give advice in strong terms regarding their return to heathen practices, and Mauga, by his candid manner, showed that he had appreciated the spirit in which reproof was given. In the afternoon, there was an examination of all the children of Mr. Powell's school, who acquitted themselves very creditably, and executed some pretty dances, or rather series of graceful simultaneous motions. The latter, however, I did not see, having accompanied Captain Cator and Mr. Williams to Leato's, by water, in a boat manned by natives, singing merrily as they vigorously paddled along.

After a long talk, the matter was arranged by that chief agreeing to pay 100 dollars, as compensation for the destruction of the boat, which had been destroyed by a war party who used violence and threatening menaces to the crew, one being a European and a British subject. No doubt the tabu had been infringed ; but the people had no means of knowing that it existed, and had actually received a hospitable reception at the village from the relatives of the dead chief, the disturbance of whose spirit these belligerents thought to appease by the outrage.

These people have suffered much from the war with Mauga's tribe. The house we went to was newly finished, being built upon the site occupied by a larger and better one, then burnt down. The stumps of the bread-fruit and cocoa-nut trees in all directions bore witness to a severer loss than that of houses, sustained during these three miserable years.

On our way back, we went into a little bay to see a large double war-canoe built by Mauga, and used in attacking the enemies' villages on the coast. Though clumsy-looking, and apparently unsafe, these vessels sail very fast, and seldom meet with serious catastrophes. They are very wet, baling-out being an incessant operation. The larger canoe is seventy feet long, and about five feet deep, built in the usual Samoan fashion, with pieces of wood of irregular sizes and shapes; the lesser canoe serving as an out-rigger, fifteen feet shorter, and of much smaller dimensions every way. Over both is a strong deck, having accommodation for 100 men; there are holes through this for paddles to be worked between the two boats; and on it a house thatched, with cooking-place, and other conveniences. Over all is a small platform upon which the chief sits, exposed to wind and weather. The masts and yards are very heavy, as are the cumbrous sails of cocoa-nut matting, which, however, they manage with great dexterity, and which are so efficient that this canoe sailed round a vessel in which the consular agent was a passenger, going eight knots. When attacking a fort, they have around the deck a high bulwark of cocoa-nut stems, loopholed for musketry.

Bread-fruit Tree.

## CHAPTER IX.

### TUTUILA.

*2d July.*—We spent the forenoon of this day at the chief's, who had several visitors whilst we were there. When strangers arrive, they enter and take their seats in silence, which, after a few minutes, is broken by mutual complimentary speeches. To-day, after a little general conversation, the clapping of hands announced that the ava was ready; and after it had been handed round, the visitors left to see H.M.S. "Fawn," the cynosure of all eyes, first shaking hands all round. The principal chiefs in Samoa have, like great men in Europe in olden times, their fools, or privileged jesters. So far as I had an opportunity of judging of these *vales*, they are most offensive rascals. Their chief recommendation is making hideous noises, and taking insolent liberties, which would cost others their lives, such as walking over the chief's legs, snatching his food from before him, and so on. They are a very peculiar-looking race, and all come from the same village in Upolu, where, for generations, they have been trained in impudence from their youth, to fit them for their calling. As they are privileged, and under Tabu, they are useful in carrying messages to hostile tribes, one of these fellows being the bearer of Mauga's letter to Leato the other day, for which service he took payment by making himself particularly odious this morning.

We came round to Leone in the evening. Loud were the shouts of "Tofa," good-bye, from the fleet of canoes, in which our friends saw us off from Pago-Pago.

Before leaving, an old Savage-island man at the mission brought in three or four immense ou-ous, which evinced, in their efforts to escape, bursting the coils of cocoa-nut sinnet, a strength quite sufficient to husk the toughest cocoa-nut. As to their method of obtaining the contents afterwards, every native (both Samoans and Niuans) confirms the account mentioned before. The Niuans understand their habits best; and the old man who brought these to-day, dug them out of the holes in which they remain many weeks torpid. The female differs from the male in having three flippers, well furnished with strong hairs, on the right side of the sac.

Mr. Hunkin's whale-boat came off as usual, and we again enjoyed going merrily in, to the song about the Man-a-wa-ohi, of her crew, as with most impassioned gesture they urged her through the sounding surf. His eldest daughter's marriage to the Samoan chief is to take place to-morrow, on board the "Fawn." There is a good deal in the father's argument (Leato, as he now calls himself, having accepted a Samoan name) that the Kannakas are much superior in every respect to the generality of Europeans in these parts; and that if a girl is to marry in Samoa, she is likely to be happier with a native, notwithstanding that, in accepting the hand of a chief, she must be generally what in other countries would be deemed a second wife. In this case, I cannot but feel sorry that the girl, gentle and amiable-looking as she is, should be married to a far from pleasant-looking native, who is already notorious for his mercenary matrimonial arrangements, and perhaps only asks her hand for the sake of her dower of fine mats.

*3d July.*—In the morning, we took the accompanying likeness of the bride and her bridesmaids, who in very handsome native dresses, wearing most elaborate trains, looked very captivating. A crowd of people came off to the ship, to see firing at a

Fr. a Photog. by Commander R. P. Cator R.N.

W & A K Johnston Edin^r

BRIDE AND BRIDESMAIDS

target with shot and shell, and then came the bridal party. The ceremony was performed with due formalities, and the bride signed her name with a firm hand, but she looked quite pale, and her interesting English features wore the expression of resignation rather than of happiness.

It is, however, she says, her own choice, and her husband declared his solemn intention to live with her for life; while the old chief, his father, who came to express his great pleasure that the ceremony was to be performed, pledged his word for his son's good behaviour. Next week all the family will go down to the husband's village, and take with them the great Tonga of mats; when two hundred pigs will be killed, and there is to be great feasting. In a marriage now-a-days, the ancient extraordinary ceremonies are not practised, but those existing under Mosaic law are still in force.

In this case the addresses were not made by proxy, as usual with Samoan chiefs, the young man having been living at his bride's father's for six months prosecuting his own suit.

*4th July.*—We left Leone last evening with a fine breeze, the Consul's difficulties in Tutuila being all arranged; and we steamed this morning into Saluafato Bay, which is superior as a harbour to the neighbouring one of Apia, being formed in the same manner by an entrance through the fringing coral reefs; but vessels entering would do well to have a native pilot, if Wilkes' charts are not on board, as there is a dangerous shoal off the entrance. We were received on the beach by Mr. Bullamacow, whose appearance is worthy of the appellation he has assumed. Bull-headed and truculent-looking, he amused himself as we walked along, by frightening all the small boys and girls who crowded too near, by shouting at them fiercely, and brandishing his club. This man has considerable influence in Upolu and also in Tutuila, as before mentioned. He accompanied us to Lufi-Lufi, about a mile and a half farther along the beach, where Tui-Atua, the king, as he considers himself, of all Samoa, lives. Tu Pua or Puli-Puli, a chief who came as passenger from Leone in the Captain's cabin, denies his authority, as many others do, though they give him the precedence, so far as rank goes. The Consul's business here was to inquire into an assault of a grave nature, said to have been committed upon the son of an Englishman, by one of the king's people.

After we had waited some time in the Fala-tele, his Majesty made his appearance, in a faded frock-coat, covered with tawdry tinsel lace, and a large crucifix and gilt chain round his neck, given him by the priests.

One cannot avoid being struck with the great difference in features and appearance altogether between the chiefs and the common people. Tui-Atua looks much more like an old Spaniard or Portuguese than a Samoan. He took his seat in silence on the royal mat; a space of about ten feet around his Majesty's squattage being free from intrusion. Among other marks of the respect and deference paid him, we observed that any canoe passing whilst we were sitting in "fono," was pushed across the shallow bay by its occupants, who waded up to their shoulders in the water. That portion of the lagoon opposite a chief's residence is considered his private domain; and fierce quarrels have often arisen in consequence of white men imprudently daring to pull their boats across the tabooed water without permission.

The conversation was carried on entirely by his orator, who seemed to have not only all the talking to himself, but also the power to make such arrangements as might appear necessary, from the turn the conversation might take, in reference to disputes of the kind under inquiry. In this case the accused having taken himself off to the other side of the island, is to be brought back here for a trial before the "Fawn" returns from Savaii. We called upon Tui-Atua afterwards at his house, a most uncomfortable-looking place on the other side of the Malai or public square, which is remarkable for three splendid Marie trees, under whose shade is the assembly-room of the village belles and cavaliers. We saw the den built up in the roof, into which he creeps at night for security, his henchman sleeping at the foot of the ladder; an attempt to murder him having been made, he said, not long ago. He lives a solitary bachelor life, which is scarcely to be wondered at, as he could not well expect that even for the honour of being wife of the great man, any fair Kannaka would consent to climb up the pole, and sleep in that dark cage. He is a Roman Catholic, and it was reported generally this morning, that he had given his support to a movement commenced at the instance of the priests, to petition for the protectorate of the Samoan group being accepted by France. "Old fool," Tu Pua said; "he had better take care what he is about!"

In the evening we returned to Apia, and found that a meeting had been convened, to which the proposal had been submitted; but one of the first native speakers, himself a Roman Catholic, having compared foreigners to bird-catchers, who endeavour by the temptation of a few stale crumbs to entice the birds within the circle of the noose, the French commander, who had no wish to have anything to do with the Samoans in any way, justly irritated, left the assembly, and so all ended in smoke. Nothing further has as yet been heard of King George's movements.

I met this afternoon a chief from Niua-foo, who came to ask for a passage in the "Fawn," thinking she was bound to Tonga. He had several joints of his fingers amputated, as marks of grief for friends deceased, the custom being common in all the islands where the Tongans have established themselves.

*5th July.*—We rode out to-day on one of the little, active, island-bred horses, some miles into the country. The road, or rather pathway, led us through a most luxuriant forest of cocoa-nut, bread-fruit, and orange trees, mingled with bananas; underneath, in the moist shade, flourished a rank growth of pine-apples, red-peppers, etc. After a mile or two, these plantations, as they are called, gave place to larger forest-trees, conspicuous among which was the beautiful banyan, out and in amongst whose feathery branches sailed the boatswain-birds in their snowy plumage, looking almost transparent against the bright rays of the tropical sun. We reached a picturesque village with open glades, in which a few cattle were feeding, giving life to the scene. Through it ran a sparkling little river, now rushing swiftly among the basaltic rocks in its bed, at the foot of high cliffs, over which hung beautiful tree-ferns, and frequently leaping in bright cascades over the dykes of lava, from fifty to a hundred feet high, over which the native girls rejoice to plunge themselves. Nothing can be more romantic and charming to the eye than the scenery in these islands, which, however, possess a climate altogether undesirable as a residence for Europeans.

We intended to have visited the Lake Lauto, an old crater, situated at an elevation of 2500 feet above the sea; but, unfortunately, we were prevented from doing so.

*6th July.*—During the last day or two, the weather, although very hot, has been much fairer than any we have experienced during the month. This has been a most truly lovely day, and the appearance of the hills and country in the clear atmosphere is certainly most inviting. Walking round the shores of the bay in the morning, we met large numbers of natives, well dressed, chiefly in white cotton serangs, returning from church at a neighbouring village; the large one here, burnt some time ago, being in process of being rebuilt. Even at Apia, where the example set by the Europeans is anything but commendable, as in most seaports, the natives observe the day in the strictest manner.

*7th July.*—I accompanied Captain Cator and Mr. Williams in a boat manned by natives, fifteen miles along the coast to Leulo Moego, where the Consul wished to have the influence of the Captain's presence, to settle the payment of a fine imposed for maltreatment of a European, some time ago.

We found the chief of the place mourning for his sister, who had just died, and therefore not visible. His people, however, met at the native teacher's house, and after some argument on the part of the talking-man with Mr. Williams, arranged for the immediate payment. This system of fining is bad, but it is difficult to substitute any other punishment at present, in the disorganized state of the island government. If the fine levied upon the chief and his people is not paid, they expect punishment when a ship of war comes; but always thinking that contingency remote, they delay as long as possible, so that in the end the fine often falls to be paid by innocent people.

Mr. Williams hopes shortly to have a proper prison erected at Apia, when the punishment inflicted upon Europeans and natives may be properly carried out.

At this place is the printing establishment of the London Mission, by means of which they have effected such great results in these islands, and others in the Western Pacific. At present, Mr. Ella being obliged to leave in ill health, the buildings seem to have got into a rather dilapidated state; as in the school-houses and other places of the kind, the white ant is rapidly carrying on the work of destruction. Much has been accomplished, however. This month an excellent dictionary of the Samoan language has been published, and the Bible has been completely translated into that and the Niuan dialect. The binding of the books, and other operations, are now entirely under the direction of a little native Æsop. I may here remark the great frequency of this deformity in Samoa; but these hunchbacks seem generally very merry, and, like "naturals" in Scotland, are the care of the village.

In the evening, we visited Malua, where there is a large college for training teachers. The establishment, it was said, had been for some time in rather a languishing condition; but it now appears quite the reverse, under the energetic superintendence of the Rev. Mr. Nisbet, who with his colleague, Mr. Turner (now absent in England), had a very narrow escape some time ago at Tanna. Each distinguished himself on that trying occasion by the greatest courage; and the modest manner in which Mr. Nisbet told us the story showed the true heroism of the man. Both these gentlemen's wives were there at the time, and though they evinced no fear of death even under such circumstances, their danger must have aggravated the temptation to comply with the entreaties of their small band of friends, that they should use their muskets against the host of savages who surrounded them. True to their principles, however, they resisted that temptation to the last; though driven back upon the shore, wet and weary, after pulling for hours hopelessly against a heavy gale, in their endeavour to escape. The natives had been incited by their priests or "medicine men," to put to death the "bringers of disease," as they termed the missionaries; and but for the timely arrival of a ship in the bay next day, which carried them off, they would no doubt have fallen victims to the superstitious fury of their enemies.

Believing, as these savages do, in the power of the priests of their own gods to cause and cure diseases, it is easy to imagine how violent their feelings must have been against the teachers of the new religion. The measles had broken out on the island, and the people died in hundreds. Whole villages were depopulated, not one being left to tell the story of their miserable end. So virulent was the disease, that in many houses, father, mother, and children all lay dead or dying at the same time, none being able to render the other any assistance; while, strange to say, the village where the missionaries had taken up their abode alone, of all in the island, totally escaped the visitation.

There are now about a hundred scholars at Malua; and as is observed among the teachers, care and regular habits make a great difference in appearance between these young men and their countrymen. They are apt scholars, and anxious to gain information, geography being one of the most favourite studies. The buildings form a square, and the dilapidated wooden cottages are being replaced by substantial structures built of stone and lime by the students themselves during certain hours, those living on one side of the square vying in skill and industry with their neighbours opposite.

A village has sprung up in the neighbourhood occupied by the fathers and mothers of the lads, with their families.

The institution is a most valuable one; and much as has been done by the native teachers in the different islands, there remains more to be accomplished by their means, which can be done by no other hands, amongst the savage cannibals of the northern and western groups, in climates still more unsuited to Europeans than the Navigators or even the New Hebrides.

We returned by moonlight, as soon as there was water enough over the coral reefs, and reached Apia at two o'clock in the morning. Our light-hearted crew relieved their toil with the usual songs, in which all joined with the exception of one,—Peter, an excellent fellow, but who, having travelled and seen the world, on the banks of the Murray River, evidently considered himself a superior being! He had been there with Captain Cadell when he first attempted the navigation of that great Australian canal, the Darling river, now open to steamers for 1500 miles from the sea.

# CHAPTER X.

## SAVAII.

*8th July.*—Having left Apia this morning at sunrise, at 3 P.M. we reached Matauto, the only tolerable harbour in Savaii. This is the largest island of the Samoan group, but is not quite so populous as Upolu, the inhabitants being estimated at 12,000. The coast is generally precipitous, and there are few anchorages for vessels of any size. The coral reef does not encircle its coasts so regularly as in the other islands; and there is reason for supposing that this is partly to be attributed to a considerable subsidence having taken place, at a comparatively recent epoch, in the bed of the ocean to the south-west of the island, and of a considerable portion of its once larger area. Volcanic eruptions have, at no distant date, much altered the features of the country. A very old man, who died lately, related to my informant the stories he had heard of the ruin caused by the outburst when he was a child.

An immense flood of lava was poured out from a crater twelve miles from Matauto over a great extent. The surface of the scoriæ and lava still uncovered by vegetation is very rough and broken, and so dangerous from crevices, that many persons have lost their lives in attempting to cross. The natives say the crater from which these fiery streams issued is of no great diameter, but very deep, and its sides so loose and perpendicular that it is impossible to descend into it. So inaccessible is the country in the neighbourhood, that its situation was only discovered a few months ago accidentally by a party of wild pig hunters.

A large carpet snake was obtained to-day; it is harmless, and considered a delicacy by the Savaiians. It is very common in this island, but rare in Upolu and Tutuila. This is the only species of land serpent known in the group. Indeed, centipedes are the only noxious creatures in Samoa.

A considerable difference in complexion and feature, as also in the dialect of the people of this part of the island, is attributable, Mr. Pratt, the missionary, informed me, to the circumstance of a colony of Fijians having settled here. They drove the natives back by force; and it is only of late years that the direct descendants of the inhabitants of the village have returned. It is singular that their neighbours should not have assisted them to expel the intruders, whose descendants still speak with awe of Tui-Viti, King of Fiji, whom they worshipped as a god, and regard still as king of men. But in Savaii, the feuds between the different districts seem to have been carried to a great excess; and it is almost surprising that, as in Tanna and New Caledonia, the dialects have not become more distinct. Now they are thorough Republicans here, and the government is patriarchal in form. Though they do not refuse to the chiefs of old families the ceremonious respect and precedence due to mere rank, they allow them but little real power.

*9th July.*—No canoe came off this morning or yesterday afternoon, the natives being afraid to venture near the guns of the "Fawn," until they knew how things are going to turn out with them, having a great fear of offending the Papalangis, since the visit of the "Cordelia," two years ago. On that occasion a murderer was given up here, and hanged at her yard-arm, but not before one of their villages had been burned, and much property destroyed,—among other things a fine war canoe, over the relics of which they mourned with tears. On the present occasion, happily, they have not much cause for fear, as it is evident that the principal men have been most anxious to prevent any cause of offence being given by any of their people, who have generally acted with great forbearance towards the white men, and more scrupulous honesty than has been shown to them in return. There is a vessel lying ashore on the reef, wrecked here some time ago, which no Kannaka has ever been on board of, in consequence of a stringent order given by the influential men. In what other part of the world could such an example of subordination and honesty be found?

At ten o'clock I accompanied the Captain and Mr. Williams to the Fala-tele, the Rev. Mr. Pratt, the energetic clergyman of the mission, coming with us, inquiries having to be made into the truth of the various complaints, lodged by Europeans with the Consul, of assaults and robberies committed by the Savaiians.

Our visit occasions great excitement; and by daylight this morning we saw from the ship a stream of people coming towards the village, from east and west. The court sat until four o'clock; the crowd was dense, inside and around the house, and we were heartily glad when the business was concluded, the heat being very oppressive, crowded up as we were by hundreds of persons redolent of cocoa-nut oil. The chief causes of dispute were about this article of commerce, obtained by the traders and not duly paid for. The Kannakas had, in consequence, according to their own custom, helped themselves, in some instances, to the debtors' property, but, as far as was proved, taking less than the actual value due to them. The discourse turned to-day, however, chiefly on pigs, and the trespasses of young grunters of an inquisitive disposition, which had broken through fences and paid the penalty with their lives. Then came the untimely death of some fat porker, by mistake, which the owner insisted on being returned alive, not slung between two poles; and divers porcine histories were recounted, which, in some way, had led to the brandishing of clubs and handling of muskets. *Cave canem* in Samoan means "Ware pig." It must have been in these islands that the nursery rhyme originated—

> "One little pig went to market;
> One little pig stayed at home," etc.—

as upon the fate of many a little pig have depended the peace and lives of its owners. The destruction of any animal found in an enclosed plantation is a very rigid custom by the Samoans; but the European settlers seemed to think that their pigs ought to be exempted from the penalties, and have the same license as their owners appear to take in all things. Pig is a term of great reproach when applied to a man, and any one using it is subject to a heavy fine; if to a chief, fifty of the said animals is the usual penalty. These good-for-nothing fellows, however, who had for years received kindness and hospitality from the people among whom they have chosen to settle, are in the habit of using it, with the most opprobrious adjectives in addition, to whom they think fit; and on their own admission it is only surprising that some of them are alive at this day. The result of the investigations to-day was that the natives, though they had committed themselves on one or two occasions,—for which fines were imposed and paid,—were not nearly so much in fault as the Europeans, who received a severe lecture, and were, to their surprise, made to pay their debts to the Kannakas.

It is hoped that the effect of the visit of the "Fawn" will be to induce the people of Savaii to adopt, as they have promised to do, the code of laws which the Consul is endeavouring to establish in Upolu, as they see that it is the anxious wish of the English to do justice impartially, and to advance the native interests. In the middle of the proceedings a great bustle and confusion commenced suddenly in the Malai, some people rushing into the Fala-tele, and seizing their spears. In front of us during the day had sat the "Rising-Moon," the lady of highest rank, and the belle of Matauto. Tu-Pua, who had come from Apia in the "Fawn," and who bears the sobriquet of the "Silver," was a suitor for her hand, and it turned out that his rival was here in the neighbourhood, with a large retinue, who, in a cowardly manner, rushed into the village with the intention of driving him off the field, if no more. They found no Tu-Pua, however, the "Rising Moon" having sent him a note as soon as he landed, telling him she did not wish him to come into the village until the evening, without giving any reason, or informing her messenger (the retainer), whom Tu-Pua had living in his family's house to sing his praises, according to Samoan custom. Tu-Pua had, accordingly, returned on board, and we did not see what otherwise, in all probability, we should have done — a pitched battle, as all the Matauto people preferred him to his rival, and would have taken up arms in his cause. We left just as the general feasting was about to commence. With loud shouts, about a hundred of the inhabitants of the village came into the Malai, bringing each a basket of provisions for the strangers, a herald who walked in front, proclaiming the name of each person for whom the various presents were intended.

Having dined at the missionaries' house, where, of course, having talked of pig all day, roast pork, as everywhere in Samoa, formed the *pièce de résistance,* we sailed again in the evening for Apia. Our friend Tu-Pua, poor fellow, came with us, without ever having seen the object of his present adoration. He seemed, however, quite sure of success, and says he will return, in a week or two, in a large canoe, and take home the "Rising-Moon" as his wife, this time really intending to be married for life. On the fifty previous occasions in which he has figured as bridegroom, the chief consideration seems to have been the exchange of property, and acquisition of fine mats. The passion for fine mats is a serious matter for a man with a number of female relations, and especially extravagant sisters, whose requirements must be provided for at all hazards, lest he should receive a sister's curse,—the direst calamity which, in the opinion of these superstitious people, can befall a man.

The inhabitants of Savaii are wealthier than their neighbours, making much cocoa-nut oil, and receiving a considerable revenue from tatooing. The most expert artists in this trade are now to be found in this island, in consequence of the objection to the practice, as a relic of heathenism, by the missionaries, who in other places, where they have more influence through the Christian chiefs, have almost put a stop to the custom. The young men come from the different parts of the group here to be thus ornamented, and very often remain permanently. The population of Manu'a is likely to be reduced from this cause, as those who indulge in the fashion are forbidden by the law to return.

The same influence prevents the custom from being carried on at Tonga; and the youth from these islands also come in large numbers for the purpose of being thus decorated, *more majorum,* without which they would be considered boys, prevented from marrying for years, not allowed to speak in the presence of grown men, and obliged to perform menial offices. The objection of the missionaries to this species of dandyism is on account of the dissipation which generally attends the operation amongst all the friends of the lads undergoing it, who assemble from far and near, and pass a time of great festivity and rioting—a perfect saturnalia —similar to that of the Australian natives, when they congregate to make young men, and the front tooth is knocked out. No regular charge is made; but, according to the rank of the family, presents of fine mats are offered to the operators. The marking is effected with a little instrument resembling a miniature rake, made of human bone, the lamp-black made from the candle-nut being rubbed in as a pigment; so closely is the skin punctured, that the original colour is not visible, except where lines are left to produce the pattern. Considerable pain and inflammation ensue, not so great as that caused by the Maori method, but so much that it can only be done in patches at a time; and, consequently, a number of lads acquainted with each other are undergoing the operation together.

The people here are very much disinclined to undertake anything that involves much trouble; and an offer of four or five pounds was not sufficient to induce any one to go the mountains to try and get a Manu-Moa, which bird is still to be found in Savaii, two having been killed within the last few months not far from Matauto.[1]

[1] From the descriptions obtained here, I am more inclined to think this bird must resemble the pigeon in appearance. Possibly, it may be a representative of the Megapodes. The Savaiians call it Manu-Moa —*fine bird;* Moa signifying a bird all over Polynesia, and being used by the Maories, without an adjective, to denote the greatest of the feathered race.

They are, however, fond of the sport of fishing, and are more expert and adventurous than their neighbours, going out far to sea in their large canoes to catch dolphins. These they take with a hook of native manufacture, baited with a flying-fish, first obtained with a hook and line, attached to a small buoy, numbers of which they leave as they sail out in the morning to be picked up on their return. Sometimes on these fishing expeditions, two or three canoes keeping together, they go out of sight of land ; and no doubt in this way numbers of them have made unintentional migrations to distant islands.

Matauto is one of the places where the pulolo is obtained in large quantities. The Samoan year is divided into two seasons: the Vae-toe-alau, or season of the south-east trade-wind, and the Vae-pulolo, or the season of rains, marked at its commencement by the arrival of the pulolo. In appearance, this highly esteemed article of food is like a white or sometimes a greenish worm, almost transparent, about twelve to eighteen inches in length, and full of small eggs. At a certain time every year it makes its appearance in such prodigious numbers as to make the water in the opening of the reef (from which they rise undoubtedly, not being seen to seaward), of quite a whitish colour, and gelatinous. The natives are very fond of eating it raw, holding it as the Italians do maccaroni. The Europeans also use it thus with pepper and salt, its flavour resembling that of an oyster, but it is generally preferred baked in a plantain leaf, in which state it becomes quite hard, and is kept from one season to another. If a single pulolo be placed upon a sheet of paper, in a few hours nothing is to be seen but a little dust, being in fact the eggs, which are each about the size of a pin-head. It is probably the spawn of some creature in a gelatinous tube, although it is asserted that the worm has an independent power of motion, and that when severed each portion continues to wriggle about for some time. One or two individuals appear on the first day, on the next the main body arrives, and on the fourth not one is to be seen. If the moon is full after the 14th of October, the pulolo is sure to come on the first day of the last quarter of that month. If previously, then its arrival will not take place until the first day of the last quarter of the November moon. All agree in confirming the assertion that it never makes its appearance on any other day but that, either in October or November. Three days before its arrival, the malio, or land-crabs (the *Gegarcinus*) are seen marching down from the mountains to the sea in myriads. They proceed in regiments straight a-head, no obstacle diverting them to the right or to the left. If a village is in their route, they go through the houses, and the natives who consider them a delicacy, have their dinners marching up to their ovens of their own accord.

So certain is the sequence, that the people in the inland villages calculate on being at the coast three days after the crabs to catch pulolo. I concluded that this substance must be their spawn, but the suggestion did not meet with acceptance, either from natives or Europeans. The former confidently assert that the crabs deposit their spawn in the woods near the banks of streams, after their return from the sea, and devour the greater part of it themselves. But as they allow that they go into salt water for a few minutes, and come up, they say, holding their sacs high up from the ground, no doubt the Samoan species, like its congener elsewhere, visits the water to wash off its spawn, which the current carries out into the openings in the reefs, where it is usually obtained in situations nearly opposite the mouth of some fresh-water stream. Mr. Consul Williams promised me to take means to ascertain next season whether the pulolo is not found in other parts of the coast, as, of course, if it is only to be seen in the particular spots mentioned by the Samoans, on the east coast, some other explanation of the phenomenon must be sought for, as the crabs go down to all the different parts of the island; and possibly it may prove, on examination, to be an annelidan of a new species. With regard to the regularity of its appearance, one can only account for it by concluding that there is a proper time and season for the crabs as well as for other animals, and that in particular years, when the state of the atmosphere is affected by the longer continuance of the dry season, their period of torpor in their burrows is prolonged.

Between Savaii and Upolu there are two other small islands, Manono and Apolima. Manono is remarkably rich and fertile, even when compared with the adjacent larger islands, upon which nature's choicest gifts have been so bountifully bestowed.

It was the head-quarters, as before mentioned, of the Malo for generations; and possessed another peculiar interest in the eyes of the Kannaka race, who believed it to be one of the resting-places or stepping-stones used by the spirits of the departed on their passage to the other world,—the Fafa-a, or entrance to which was by either of two circular hollows at the west end of Savaii. From a rock lying off the end of Upolu, which served them first to take a flying leap into the sea, they swam to Manono, where they rested a while, after which a second jump was taken from a rock off its shore, whence they swam to Savaii. It is remarkable how similar ideas have been held by people of the different races in these regions; and another proof is afforded of the mixture of the two in almost all the principal groups and islands of Polynesia and Melanesia. At Fiji, Admiral Erskine mentions that a certain promontory named "Dimba-Dimba, at Bua Bay, is considered a place of peculiar sanctity, being that from which spirits were supposed to depart for the judgment-seat of the powerful god Dengei, who resides, in the form of a *huge serpent*, in the neighbourhood of Nakauvandra." Near Apolima, the little island fortified by nature and art, in the vicinity of Manono, lives the sacred Eel of the Samoans, a huge monster, "the devourer of men," according to the fables of these superstitious people, one of whose "aitus," or tutelary deities, the eel was formerly considered. In the little river of Pago-Pago there were formerly great numbers of large ones. Since the introduction of Christianity, these myths are no longer believed in by the natives, who now eat their gods without any scruple, and only sigh when they speak of them, and remember how capital they were, baked in a plantain-leaf. Some of these fresh-water eels are enormous. Mr. Williams saw one caught which was nine feet long, and as thick as a lad's body. Sharks and turtles also were sometimes worshipped as aitus. It is alleged that they were tamed at times from being constantly fed at accustomed places. Between Pago-Pago and Leone there is a little bay where there still live two, which come in when called upon in the name of an old famous chief. The consular agent said he had thrice seen the shark, at all events, come sailing in from the reef when shouted for. Probably if any one watched there any day, for an hour at a time, some of his relatives would also make their appearance.

## CHAPTER XI.

### SAMOA.

11*th July.*—We steamed into Saluafato Bay this afternoon according to tryst, the heavy rains which we have had since leaving Matauto having beaten down the wind and sea, against which we tacked about for twenty-four hours. We found that the natives charged with the assault had been secured by the chiefs, who were assembled waiting for the arrival of the "Fawn." The Englishman, the father of the lad beaten (who in features and complexion seemed a pure Kannaka), was suffering from a severe fit of the country fever, from repeated attacks of which his legs and arms were swollen to a most fearful size. Mr. Williams received a letter from Apia, mentioning that dysentery had been very prevalent since we left, several deaths having taken place. This disease has lately swept off a large number of people at Fiji; and if this wet season continues, its ravages are to be dreaded here.

The natives attributed its appearance to infection brought by a vessel which came from that group of islands ten days since, now lying in Apia harbour, having on board, preserved in spirits, the body of its late owner, who died of this malady.

Tu-Pua went on shore to see his friends. Many came up and shook hands with him in a respectful manner, and at the same time affectionately, some lifting his hand to their lips, others touching noses. One nice-looking child, his niece, came running up, and kissed him joyfully, or rather smelt him, for the mode of salutation more resembles that of the Maories than our English one.

The ship was surrounded by a great fleet of canoes, and the usual merry laughing testified that her coming here to punish an offender did not interfere with the general satisfaction caused by the arrival of an English man-of-war. This village was burnt down some years ago, by the American squadron under Commodore Wilkes, in consequence of their refusal to give up the murderer of an American citizen. The natives begin fully to appreciate the justice of our laws, which do not permit the innocent to be sacrificed on behalf of the guilty, as was formerly the case amongst the Samoans, who deem a life for a life sufficient atonement. When the "Cordelia" went to Matauto, the people endeavoured to save the guilty chief, and killed an innocent man of lòw caste, thinking that quite sufficient reparation for the death of an Englishman of ignoble blood.

The inquiry terminated as usual to-day. Provocation had been given by the lad, who called himself an Englishman, and used most insulting language to the Samoan, who was, however, fined for removing the goods of the father to reimburse himself.

Bull-a-ma-cow was sick, and did not appear before Mr. Williams (acting also as American consul at present) to answer the complaint made against him by a New York negro, who had married his daughter, for taking her and a large quantity of his goods from him. We were hospitably entertained by the chief of Salua-fato village. At Lufi-Lufi, Tua Atua did not make his appearance, so nobody called on his majesty.

On landing, I had accepted, according to Samoan fashion, the friendship of a good-natured looking matron, wife of the native teacher; and on leaving, her brother came alongside, with a present of cooked taro, fowls, and palu-sammy, shells, etc. In these cases, no doubt, the friend expects a return gift. But the mode of the offering, which is often made under circumstances where no return can be expected, speaks well for the people who evince such kindly hospitality.

Tu-Pua came down to the boat with his attendants, carrying four large live pigs, as his present to Captain Cator, articles of food being, as in Japan, the first offering of friendship. He had been fellow passenger in his cabin, with Mr. Williams and myself, for ten days, and his behaviour has always been most correct and considerate. He had his servant with him, and generally appeared well dressed in various European costumes, of which he seemed to possess an ample wardrobe. To-day, however, he came to dinner as a Kannaka chief, in his lava-lava only, apologizing, on account of the great heat, for dispensing with clothes above his waist.

He would much like to go to England. "My heart is burning," he said, "to see the world. If I had not tried to see as much of Englishmen as possible, I should have been like all the Kannakas, and have thought there was no country like Samoa."

He seemed to have a pretty good idea of the relative positions of the different countries of Europe, and asked many questions about the Crimean war.

Like Mauga, he took much interest in having all the great modern discoveries in science and art explained to him. The expression of the Tutuila chief, on hearing about the electric telegraph, was, "The Papalangis are spirits; by and by, they will catch the thoughts of a man." Tu-Pua said "the French and Russians, and other nations, are very great, but the English are so just, and fulfil what they promise so faithfully, that Providence favours them, and in the end they must rule all nations."

In the evening, the "Fawn" anchored again in Apia harbour, and we found that during the last day or two, there had been ten or twelve deaths from dysentery in the village, and the people were much alarmed.

15*th July*.—Going this morning, as usual, before sunrise, to bathe in the little river which runs into the bay, I passed a house where a number of people were assembled, singing the morning-hymn, and reading prayers, before going to work at the restoration of the church.

A large fono, or public meeting, was held to-day, at which all the chiefs of the neighbouring districts were assembled, the adoption of the proposed laws being the subject principally under debate. The expression of opinion was unanimously favourable;

and I have little doubt that if they were printed, and presented to the chiefs in the various districts, throughout the group individually, it would not be difficult to have one code established throughout Samoa.

On Sunday last, an American negro having attempted to smuggle spirits on board the "Fawn," his boat was seized and destroyed alongside, and he himself was sentenced by the chief Manutafa today to six months' banishment from Apia. These negro cooks and stewards of American ships form a considerable portion of the British and American subjects in these islands. One woolly-headed fellow, black as jet, informed us that he was the first *white man* who settled at Apia!

It was reported in the village that the Raging Bull had insolently refused to come here, and answer his son-in-law's complaint, who claims to be a British subject (from Quebec), and that he had torn up the Consul's letter, and stamped contemptuously on the pieces.

Whilst the assembly was still sitting, he arrived, however, with his retainers, and when the business was concluded, according to the requirements of etiquette, the chiefs retired for a time, taking their seats again after Bull-a-ma-cow had entered. He indignantly denied the charge; earnestly requested to be confronted with his accusers, of whatever colour they might be, and that a messenger might be sent to the king Tui-Atua's house to bring the letter. He was told by Captain Cator that his word as a gentleman was sufficient, and the matter dropped.

His daughter having been sent for, refused to rejoin her woolly-headed lord and master, whom she never liked, she said, and only married from fear of her father, who had insisted upon her doing so; and there is no doubt but the "Pawer of the ground" is not the mildest man in the world at home. To-day, nevertheless, he actually shed tears of rage and vexation at being spoken to in strong terms by the Consul before his brother chiefs, and in a strange Fala-tele. He had, however, brought all the muskets and other things which he had taken away, and they were restored to their owner, who seemed perfectly satisfied to say "Good-bye" to his wife and her father. It is well that there is a Consul here so thoroughly acquainted with the native habits and customs, and who does not hesitate to punish the chiefs even when they are in the wrong, although he, *con amore*, acts up to the wording of his commission, which enjoins "patience, forbearance, and kindness, towards the Aborigines."

A considerable amount of the first-mentioned virtue is necessary to enable one to sit out, cross-legged, a Samoan inquiry. They are excessively fond of talk; and at public meetings, hours are consumed in settling who is to speak first, and in paying compliments before the actual business is commenced.

The decisions in many of the cases which have been under investigation must have shown them that strict impartiality is maintained, and that Europeans acting improperly will meet with no consideration on account of their colour. The visit of the "Fawn" will, I have no doubt, be productive of much good, as the Kannakas see they have no reason to be jealous of their rights, which will be protected, so long as they do not transgress the rules of common justice, and act in opposition to the principles they profess.

16*th July*.—Two schooners arrived this morning from Tonga-taboo and Fiji, bringing the intelligence that King George's intended visit is not to take place, in consequence of the persuasions of Her Britannic Majesty's Consul there. To-day we said "Tofa" to the Samoans, leaving Apia harbour at sunset.

These interesting, good-humoured, and hospitable people have many virtues to counterbalance their failings; and one's feelings towards them are not influenced by the recollection that, like others in the Pacific, they were lately addicted to the most cruel customs and revolting cannibalism. They may perhaps have been so to a certain extent in remote times; but so far as their own traditions reach, they never actually had a relish for "Bakola," or human flesh. This word (literally meaning "eating food") is the only one the Fijians have to denote the human body, unless indeed when they speak of Puaka-balava, or long pig, in contradistinction to Puaka-dina, short pig. They admit that at times an enemy, notorious for cruelty and hostility, has been cooked, and a portion of the body tasted by each of his conquerors as the token of utmost detestation and triumphant vengeance. Nor did they ever practise any of the horrible cruelties of the Fijians and other Melanasians (as the islanders of the Papuan or Negrillo race are called by the French), who launched their war-canoes over the prostrate bodies of half a hecatomb of living men, used as rollers; and with each post of a new house, buried some unfortunates alive, placed in the post-holes, each standing up with his arms round the tree. Of the ferocity of these savages, no stronger illustration can be given than the lament of a chief over his son, whose many virtues and amiable qualities he enumerated in the bitterness of his sorrow, winding up with the exclamation, "Oh, my son, my son! So just, so brave, and fierce was he; if even any of his own wives disobeyed him, he cooked and ate them on the spot!"

The inhabitants of these islands used to be called by their Rarotongan neighbours the godless Samoans. But the reproach was not literally deserved. Though they had no temples or altars, and observed none of the horrid sacrificial rites practised elsewhere, they lived in the most superstitious fear of their deities, whose name was legion; so much so, that it appears they were afraid of rendering too particular service to one, lest they should offend another. "According to the number of their cities, so were their gods." Every village had its own particular one; every one his own Lares or Penates, which appeared visibly incarnate in some bird, fish, or reptile. Even the limpet on the rock was regarded by some as a divinity, and safe from injury at their hands. The coincidence between this belief and the Hindu doctrine is worthy of remark.

Their superstitious fear of the world of spirits was extreme, and still is, but not more so than that existing now-a-days amongst many persons of the most civilized nations. In their love for their parents and children, attention to the sick and dying, as well as in their respect for the memory of the dead, they are remarkable. If a friend or relative is killed or lost, and unburied, it causes them the greatest concern for the peace of his spirit, which they fancy they hear complaining at night, and saying, "So cold! oh, so cold!" No doubt it may be said that this feeling is partly caused by the fear of the aggrieved spirit's returning, and doing them injury, and that their extreme attention to the person about to enter the Fa-fa is attributable to the desire that he should do so without any ill feeling towards his survivors. A Samoan cannot understand that, in civilized England, there are actually people who have no homes, no friends, and are obliged to beg their bread.

In many of their customs and traditions a singular resemblance has been traced to those of the Israelites of old, the chief of which may be mentioned: the rite of circumcision, the maids' token, cities of refuge, burying in their own gardens, death as the punishment of infidelity, and the like.

From whatever branch of the Asiatic family they derive their descent, it is evident that many have in their veins a strong infusion of the blood of emigrants from the "Flowery Land," as well, probably, as that derived from some old Japanese vikings, whose vessels at one time "covered the seas, and spread terror along the coasts of China for thousands of miles." I saw several men who, if met anywhere else, would have been taken for Chinese, having the same oblique eyes and wearing their hair in two little twisted tails behind the ears.

The population is thought, by those likely to form a correct opinion, to be rather on the increase of late years, and is estimated at thirty-four thousand, which is perhaps not more than a third of what it once was. The cessation of feuds between the tribes is in a great measure the principal cause of the increase. One sees now great numbers of children, merry little urchins running about bare-headed in the fierce sun. To promote the growth of a fine head of hair, which most of them certainly possess, all have their heads shaved when young, the girls having a long lock left on either side over their ears, and the boys upon one side only.

The *spolia opima* we carry away of most interest are ferns, which, as might be expected in so hot and moist a climate, are a predominant feature in the vegetation, and attain great size and beauty. The corals and corallines are very handsome, and the conchologist may procure many rare specimens for his cabinet from the reefs and banks, but the Paumotus group, with the reefs fringing its hundred isles, is the place where the naturalist's researches are most rewarded.

Animals there are none, with the exception of the rousettes and rats and mice, and a small dog upon the island of Manona,—the descendant, probably, of the original companions of the first emigrants from the East. Ducks, pigeons, and dotterels are the only birds a sportsman can find to keep his hands in practice. The woods are lively, however, there being many doves, parrakeets, and small birds, some of which sing rather sweetly.

The climate of Samoa is decidedly unhealthy for Europeans. Natives even of Niue and of the Harvey group, whose latitude differs from this only some four or five degrees, suffer nearly as much as those born in more temperate climes, from the moist heat of the high volcanic islands over which the invigorating breath of the trade-winds cannot freely pass. The tops of the mountains were seldom visible during our stay, dense clouds rolling far down their sides every day. We have, however, been extremely unfortunate in experiencing so much wet weather in this, usually the driest season of the year; it would be, therefore, scarcely fair to condemn it on account of the "Fawn's" heavy sick-list, about one-fifth of the hands being now laid up, chiefly with boils however. But the ghastly appearance of most of the European residents speaks for itself, there being scarcely one not affected with Elephantiasis.

The mean temperature varies little throughout the year, the difference between that of the months of January and July being only two degrees.

Earthquakes are occasionally severe, and slight shocks are of very frequent occurrence. The motion is always from north-east to south-west. Oscillations of the sea have, at the same time, occurred occasionally. The most severe one recorded took place in September 1849, when the tide ebbed and flowed ten times in five hours, rising several feet above the level of the spring-tides.

Similar oscillations were observed in 1837, on the same day that such devastation was caused by an earthquake along the coast of South America and at the Sandwich Islands, when the sea receded to a considerable distance beyond low-water mark, and then suddenly returned in one mighty wave, sweeping all the coast with irresistible force. On the same day and hour a like phenomenon happened at Tanna, in the New Hebrides.

# CHAPTER XII.

## UEA.

17*th July.*—"Fawn's" weather again; raining and blowing; covered hatchways; heat and unpleasant odours. The delightful sailing before the balmy trade-winds among the lovely islands of the Pacific, we have hitherto found to be a myth. A very heavy swell from the south keeps us rolling heavily; seas are pouring down; fowls and pigs make startlingly rapid exits from our dinner-table; and the noise of winds and waters is varied now and then by the crashing of everything breakable, evil-disposed spirits being bent upon taking advantage of the excellent opportunity of removing all chairs and tables from their accustomed places.

Our next destination is Uea, or Wallis Island, where the "Fawn" is bound for the purpose of enforcing payment of a fine of twenty tuns of cocoa-nut oil, value about £600, inflicted by the commander of H.M.S. "Elk" upon the natives, for plundering a vessel which got ashore on the reef, and maltreating her crew. It is very necessary, no doubt, to teach these people the difference between *meum* and *tuum* under all circumstances; but one cannot help feeling sorrow for them, considering that they are only acting according to their custom *from time immemorial* (as they always say). One remembers too the right of flotsam and jetsam often ruthlessly exercised not long ago in our own island, and the savage scenes which have been enacted on the coast of Cornwall, especially; where, when a ship was reported driving on shore in the middle of service upon a certain Sunday, not a century ago, the congregation, when about to rush out of church, were imploringly entreated by the reverend pastor just to wait a few moments until he pronounced the blessing, that all might start fair. We only trust that it may be true as reported, that the fine is all ready for delivery, so that the people of Uea may have no cause to regret the visit of H.M.S. "Fawn."

18*th July.*—After another most disagreeable night of rain, pitching and rolling, with the thermometer at 90°, at eleven o'clock this forenoon sail was taken in, and the auxiliary screw put in motion off the narrow opening in the coral reef, which encircles the dominions of the Queen of Uea, or Uvea, as it is pronounced by the natives. The wind blew hard; round as far as the eye could reach, the white foam of the huge green breakers dashed high and threateningly, except in the narrow passage, about a cable in breadth, of dark blue water, fringed with boiling foam, drifted backwards by the wind high in the air. We steamed in against a strong tide, the force of which was much increased to-day by the great quantity of water pouring into the lagoon over the reef. For a time, when in the narrowest part, we scarcely seemed to hold our own, and the boldest held his breath; for although lives might not be lost, the fate of the "Fawn" was certain, if any accident had for a moment interfered with the working of her machinery. At last, slowly she moved past the portals of the reef, and entered the comparatively quiet waters of the lagoon, where two vessels, with English colours flying, lay at anchor in rather dangerous proximity to the rocks. The scenery is very remarkable, and imagination can scarcely picture the peculiar effect of the whole panorama.

Beyond the broad margin of emerald-green water over the reef, which fringed the darker edge of the lagoon, one's gaze was fascinated by the grand appearance of the heaving ocean, seemingly much higher than the rocky barrier against which its mighty waves broke in constant thunder. As it rolled on in a continuous wall of water, one thought it must pass over the defence, and sweep across the low cocoa-nut-covered islands. But it dashes harmlessly against the massive fortifications raised by those pigmy artisans, which defy its strength, and safely guard the lake-hill expanse, in which rise, covered with richest vegetation, the sixteen islands, forming the small and isolated dominion of Queen Lava-Lua.

Having steamed two or three miles up, the anchor was let go under the lee of one of the islands upon the reef itself, covered with cocoa-nuts, under the shade of which were dotted all along the beach the houses of the natives, built in Samoan fashion, but smaller. No canoes coming off, the Captain and I landed, and found them all unoccupied, a pole being planted before each, with a few nuts tied upon it, as a sign of tabu. The only living creatures visible, were multitudes of hermit-crabs. It was amusing to see walking up the trees and along the branches, sea-shells of all colours and species, each being the stolen abode of one of these robbers, which, if you approach the tree, tumble down from it at once like a shower of crab-apples. The way in which these creatures adapt themselves to their habitation is very interesting, their two larger claws forming, when retracted, a perfect operculum.

One of the "Fawn's" boats had gone off to the vessel nearest, and in the morning the principal chief of this part of the island is to pilot her up to the town where her Majesty resides. The "James" schooner, it seems, had been anchored three days ago where the "Fawn" is now, but it had blown so hard, that she had drifted with three anchors down to her present unpleasant position.

Her visit into the lagoon of Uvea had been quite unintentional. As she sailed close along the outside of the reef, with all sails set, to the light morning breeze off shore, so great was the strength of the tide, that she was drawn in, through the narrow passage, with all sails standing, against the wind! On board of her are a chief and one or two other natives of the Kingsmill group, hostages for the safety of an agent left there on a former voyage, to collect cocoa-nut oil. They came on board the "Fawn," and seemed much astonished at the sight of the guns; they had been to Sydney, and were to be landed at their native place, where it is to be hoped they may do something towards civilizing a little their negrillo countrymen ; at least in creating a less hostile feeling amongst them towards the white man than now exists.

We hear that the arrival of the "Fawn" has created great alarm, as the fine is not yet all collected, although the sale of any oil had been forbidden by the Queen, as soon as the letter from the Commodore, desiring her to have it in readiness, was received ; the two vessels now here having been unable to obtain any in consequence. In the evening, after our return from the little island, Captain Cator was unfortunately seized with a severe attack of fever.

19*th July.*—The weather is clearer and cooler ; the wind, however, still blowing very hard, but without rain. The chief, Tunghalla (John, of course, *Anglicè*), came on board early to pilot us up ;—a remarkably handsome-looking man, dressed in one of the fine mats, fringed and tufted over with red worsted stuff, and wearing a long grey beard, an ornament one seldom sees among the Samoans. He was tatooed, as he said, "according to the fashion of that country," one not much in vogue here. He spoke very good English indeed, which is the more surprising as he has never been further from his native island than the nearest one of Fotuna, distant two hundred and fifty miles, and the number of Englishmen here is very small, it being the head-quarters of the French mission, and the residence of the Roman Catholic bishop of the diocese.

Notwithstanding the errand upon which she was come, he took the ship in charge, and in the afternoon piloted her safely to the anchorage off Matauto, the cathedral town and the royal residence. The navigation is somewhat intricate, and no vessel of the same size had ever been up so far, there being many shoals and patches of coral, rendering it very difficult for a sailing ship to make the attempt. Close to the inner edge of the coral wall, which is generally about a quarter of a mile in width, we found deep water all the way. No one sailing up here, and observing this wonderful construction, could avoid coming to the conclusion that Mr. Darwin's theory of the formation of those singular lagoon islands is the correct one. One could see here in the course of formation, one or two little islands on the reef itself, with a cocoa-nut tree growing here and there, amongst the coral sand and broken shells heaped up by the winds and waves.

Perhaps at some future time the present islands may disappear from the light of day, and a new circular island upon the summit of the barrier reef, when again it has been raised up by its indefatigable builders to the surface, alone be seen. In that case, it would much resemble the island to which a colony from this have given the same name, one of the northern ones of the Loyalty group, which is thirty miles in length, and from two to three miles wide, being in the shape of a horse-shoe round its lagoon.

Tunghalla having safely brought the "Fawn" to her anchorage, a feat of which he was not a little proud, did not seem quite to like landing at the town; perhaps he felt that assisting to bring the "devil" ship here was not a very patriotic proceeding. He is rather a celebrated character in his way, and his fame as a mighty man of war had reached distant places, amongst others Fotuna; and thereby hangs a tale which I give in his own words, as he told the story himself with much gusto, and which is corroborated by persons on shore, who had been at the scene of his exploit. "Well, sit down," said he, "and I will tell you true all about it. People talk so much, half true, half lie; you won't know how much true, so I will tell you myself. Well, you see, the King of Fotuna send a message to me —'Tunghalla! I hear you great *fitea fitea* man; come, and let me see your beard. I have got a sharp razor.' So I sent him word, by and by, when I have put Uvea all right, Queen and all that, I'll show you my beard. So when things all put right here, when old King die, and I make Lava-Lua Queen, you know—for people here all do what I say them—I go with one hundred and seventy good men in a whale-ship, and two big canoes, and stopped between Fotuna and the other small island, Alofi, and sent a boat ashore with message to King Sam, as they called him, to come and look at me. He say 'too much frightened; no come.' Then I said, 'You no come and see me, I come with my men directly, and look at your razor.' Then he come and say to me, 'Tunghalla! I see you great *fitea* man; I too much frightened. I give you my country; my land yours.' 'What for give me land,' I say, 'before fight? You fight me first, and give me country after, and then I'll be king, if I beat; what for so stupid, and give land before?' But he put his face between his hands, and cry and say, 'Tunghalla, I give you my country.' So I say, 'Thank you, sir, very much obliged indeed.' So I take it, and live there one year, then tired, and want to come back to Uvea; so I leave Fotuna, and bring King Sam with me."

This he did, and treated him hospitably for some

months, and then paid his passage back in a whaler, and sent the restored monarch to his island liberally supplied with presents.

The Captain being unable to go on shore, no communication took place with Her Majesty of Uvea; and as to-morrow is our Sunday, and next day theirs (which is correct time here), some time must elapse before the people, who are in great trepidation, can be relieved from their anxiety, as there is no doubt they will be. So far as reports have been received, it appears that there is another case, in which the bad conduct of the natives has been exaggerated, and the provocation received by them not considered. Indeed, so much is this the case, that one cannot avoid arriving at the conclusion that there must have been very slight investigation of the circumstances, before the heavy fine of thirty-three tuns of oil was imposed by the Commander of H.M.S. "Elk," who had been deceived by the false statements of the complainant.

*20th July.*—This afternoon I went on shore with Mr. Medley, the First Lieutenant, who took to the Queen a letter from the Captain, and one also from the Commodore, demanding immediate payment of the fine, with an allusion to the presence of H.M.S. "Fawn," which could not well be misunderstood, though the terms in which they were couched were, of course, most polite, and duly ceremonious.

On landing, it may be supposed we were not received with smiles of welcome. The men passed by civilly, with many " alofas," but with cold looks, whilst the ladies of the Matauto scarcely even looked at us; or if they honoured us so much, from motives of curiosity, our attempts at a pleasant "How do you do?" were returned with a defiant stare. We went up to the Queen's palace, which was a house of moderate size, built upon the Samoan model, standing by itself, near the large and handsome stone church (the cathedral). The old lady, Fala-Kika Lava-Lua, received us politely, seated upon one or two folded tapas, with one round her waist, and a not very elegant dimity upper garment; one or two elderly *maids of honour* were on either side of her, whilst a large assembly of the principal men of the place sat cross-legged around, on their mats as in Samoa. The house was quite full, a respectful distance, however, being kept from the Queen, who is treated with great deference and respect, though her power in some matters is more nominal than real.

The letter having been read and interpreted, she appeared pleased with the tone of respect and consideration; but said it was very hard indeed that she should be so severely punished under the circumstances, when she had done her best to prevent the claimant, a person named Delaney, from suffering loss, and that a fine of £500 should be expected for goods that were not worth more than £10. She admitted that some things had been taken which had been washed off from the vessel; but that she had, as soon as she heard of it, ordered them to be restored; that this had been done; and that it was quite false that the crew had been maltreated. On the contrary, that they had been taken off by her own people in their canoes, and fed and lodged in their houses, and that the vessel was lost by the captain's own fault, who refused to take a pilot, threatening to flog old Tunghalla, who had offered his services. His people were naturally irritated at the man's conduct to their chief; laughed at and jeered him when he got his vessel into danger; and had refused to render any assistance, beyond saving the lives of the crew. She was informed that all that she said would be repeated to the Captain of the Queen of England's ship; and as we left, she presented a piece of dry kava, which is the greatest mark of respect, as a token, no doubt, of her appreciation of the deference shown to her.

One could not but be struck with the self-possession and determination of manner of the old woman. She did not consult with or receive any advice from her *prime minister*, who was present, but took all the talking upon herself, and appeared quite contented and willing to have continued the conversation for an indefinite period, if we had not bowed ourselves out of the presence.

No doubt the conduct of Englishmen must strike people such as these we are amongst as cool, to say the least of it, knowing that their visitors have come to enforce (under the terror of the guns and rocket-tube of the "Fawn") what must doubtless seem to them a most unjust and ungrateful imposition (in which opinion no honest person can differ from them). It must appear rather extraordinary to see one or two men land on their shores, and walk about singly wherever they had a mind, as if certain to be safe and welcome anywhere.

At the back of the town, which is fortified by a deep moat and loop-holed walls, there is a prettily situated enclosed burial ground. Many of the graves are marked by tomb-stones and crosses, and they are covered generally with white coral sand. Close by runs the main highway across the island, broad and well kept, and shaded pleasantly

Fr. a Photg. by Commander R.P. Cator R.N.

W & A K. Johnston Edin^r

HOUSE AT UEA

with rows of cocoa-nut trees regularly planted. At the back are plantations of taro, yams, pandanus or screw-pine, which is here used in considerable quantities as an article of food, and also of the kava (*Piper mythisticum*), of the juice of which they seem to be considerable consumers.

We met numbers of people returning with baskets of fruit and vegetables, and other provisions for to-morrow, Sunday being strictly observed, but, as in other Catholic countries, more as a holiday; all carried large jack-knives, about twelve to eighteen inches in length, used for gardening purposes, with which they lop off the boughs as they go along, and keep the pathways always clean. The only use they made of those formidable weapons, as far as my companion or myself was concerned, was to cut and sharpen the sticks upon which they husked cocoa-nuts for us, which we summoned up impudence enough to ask for, the day being very hot.

In features the Uveans are like the Samoans, but rather darker, and with less flattened noses. Their Tongan dialect sounded much less soft and melodious than that of their neighbours, the frequent use of a hard *k* giving it a harshness which, to my ear, is not lessened by the substitution of the aspirate for *s*, and *r* for *l*. The men are seldom tatooed, and nearly all wear cotton serongs, the titi of dracæna-leaves being rarely used. The women generally have their frizzled hair hanging down upon their shoulders, and are fond of adorning their faces with yellow ochre and red paint. Yellow is, however, the fashion, in shade very similar to that of the prevailing orange-coloured ribbons now fluttering in every church.

The soil is a rich red earth like that of Savaii, and bears a dense vegetation as in the other islands. The scenery is pretty, but there is nothing grand about it, the summit alone of the ancient mighty volcano being now above water. Its seven craters, all very deep, with precipitous cliffs, are now quiet lakes of deep cool water.

21*st July.*—I went to church this afternoon, and have seldom witnessed a more impressive sight than that large and earnest congregation devoutly performing the imposing services of their religion in the fine building raised by their own hands, which to them must seem a wonderful erection, as indeed it is, being all built of well-squared blocks of vesicular lava. It reflects the greatest credit upon the venerable Bishop Bataillon, and the clergy of the French mission, by whom it was undertaken and completed.

The men and women sat cross-legged, of course, on the floor; the men on the right and the women on the left of the altar. The chanting and singing was very good indeed; the female voices, however, being much inferior to those of the men, some of whom sang an excellent tenor. The women, sitting together with their frizzled heads of hair all squared at the bottom, put me much in mind of the figures depicted upon the Nineveh marbles. In some of the islands to the westward they have a way of dressing it in a multitude of little ringlets, twisted with fine cocoa-nut twine, and the men have their beards arranged in the same manner, also cut square, giving them almost identically the same appearance with the Assyrian figures.

22*d July.*—Captain Cator having recovered sufficiently to go on shore, I went with him and Mr. Hayward, the paymaster, to the Queen's. She was in her wonted garb—chintz wrapper and tapa; the house as full of people as it could hold, and a large assemblage crowded outside. Every face wore an anxious look, as they knew that the quantity of oil was not ready, and the nuts left upon the trees being now young, it was not to be obtained, and they had heard that the non-payment would be followed by punishment, probably the destruction of their town. However, the feeling of alarm which had pervaded the island upon our arrival, and still prevents any canoes from coming off (the Queen having issued orders that none of the people should do so lest the Captain should *cut off their heads*), has perhaps a little abated, in consequence of the friendly disposition we have endeavoured to manifest towards them.

After we had squatted ourselves, a few minutes of respectful silence ensued. Then the Queen Lava-Lua, through her interpreter Solomon, who spoke both French and English a little, paid her compliments to the Captain, which were returned by him with interest. "Lilai-lilai; good, good," she said, and patted her tapa approvingly, with her three fingers, her allowance upon either hand, the others having been sacrificed, joint by joint, as tributes of affection, upon their death, to her dead relatives.

The Fono was long and wearisome, and we were glad to stretch out our legs, covering them with a mat, according to the rules of etiquette. Over and over the same ground for some time did we go. The poor old Queen could not, or would not understand that she must pay twenty tuns of oil, having made up her mind that the fine had been commuted to ten; the representative of the complainant having agreed to accept that quantity. She always recommenced with the same exordium,—"Is it possible that you have no compassion for me?" And then followed all the story over again. At last, after consultation with her advisers, during which we left the house for a time, she took the recommendation of Solomon, her principal adviser, and acceded to the Captain's demand, which it was absolutely necessary for him, in compliance with his orders, to insist upon. In consideration of the circumstance that the claimant had, like Pharaoh with the Israelites' bricks, insisted upon his oil without giving the natives any casks to put it in, and seeing there were almost no cocoa-nuts on the trees, the time for payment of the one-half was extended, and it is to be hoped that in the interim those before whom the matter may come will preserve the reputation we have in those regions for justice and honesty by remitting this portion of the cruel and unjust exaction.

The words will scarcely be deemed too strong, seeing that we found the Queen's statements confirmed by all the Europeans on the island, and that the complainant had actually opened a store with the very goods returned by the natives, and those left in his vessel, which were brought off for him, and sold them to these people, whom he represented as savage robbers.

It is one of the most flagrant cases certainly that has come under our notice, of the unfair treatment the Polynesian islanders too often experience at the hands of the Papalangis ; and in this particular instance, it is the more intolerable, when it is considered that H.M.S. "Elk" took away from Uvea thirteen shipwrecked British subjects, saved by the natives. A vessel having foundered at sea, off Savaii, the crew constructed a raft, upon which they were driven before the strong south-east wind towards this island, which they in vain endeavoured to reach. They were observed helplessly drifting past its shores by the natives, who swam out, and towed the raft through the breakers on to the reef : no slight undertaking even for Polynesian swimmers. Many of the men were so exhausted that they could not walk, and were carried by them kindly into their houses, where all the thirteen were hospitably taken care of, and supplied with all the luxuries within reach, until they were afforded the means of leaving. For this they were munificently rewarded with the sum of one dollar and a half for each man, the estimated value of an English sailor by their countrymen, who inflicted the severe penalty of nearly a year's whole produce of the island upon the people of Uvea, because one or two of them had appropriated a few dollars' worth of goods floating about the reef!

It is rather curious to us, to be under the necessity of speaking French to South Sea Islanders, some of her Majesty's chief speakers being better acquainted with that language than with English. One of her interpreters (Solomon, above mentioned) had actually been a calèche-driver for two years in Paris. When any of them addressed her in explanation of the remarks made, they leaned forward, and spoke in a low and respectful tone, in the language of ceremony. The great respect shown to women is one of the most distinguishing marks of superior civilisation of the Tongan race.

The power of the Tui-Tonga, Fa-fine, or ladies of the royal blood of Tonga, is considerable; and should a man of ignoble family marry a woman of rank, he must still, in public, pay her all the ceremonious respect and attention to which she is entitled by her birth.

22*d* *July*.—Queen Lava-Lui having requested Captain Cator to hear a complaint she had to make against the agent appointed to receive the oil, for non-payment of the duty she claims upon all exported, we went again to her house this morning. There were very few people present, only the heir-apparent, and Solomon, her French-talking chief, the *protégé* of the Pope, and quondam calèche-driver. She seemed, however, perfectly able to conduct her own business, and as anxious for the thirty dollars due to her being forthcoming, as any European emperor could be for the success of a loan wherewith to fill his impoverished exchequer.

The matter having been settled in her favour, after a long conversation regarding laws and regulations, made or to be made, the clapping of hands announced that the kava bowl was prepared, and the cup was handed round with all formality, the names of those to whom it was to be offered being announced by the eldest lady in waiting. Lava-Lui herself being, in right of her position, "incapable of doing wrong," does as she chooses, and is the only female I have ever seen taste this nasty decoction. The bowl being handed to her first, she threw it down empty, and made it twirl round on the floor, with a *dégagé* air worthy of the most experienced kava-drinking chief.

An example of the peculiar powers she possesses came under notice to-day. This European against whom the complaint was made by her, a Frenchman, was evidently in her Majesty's black books; and some time since, she placed him under taboo for six months. During that time he could buy no oil or other goods from the natives, nor dispose of any of his wares, and had difficulty in obtaining even the necessaries of life for his own subsistence, until he settled in the neighbourhood of Tunghalla's residence, who is in bad odour now at court, and whose house is open, in consequence, to those in disgrace at head-quarters.

Since the mission was first established by the brave old Bishop Bataillon, the island has been much distracted by civil war, and the strong fortifications round the principal settlements speak for themselves. At one time, a large number of fighting men came from Protestant Niua Foo, to assist their heathen cousins in putting down Catholicism, and bring the people of Matauto, who supported the missionaries, into their way of thinking, *vi et armis*. The contest was long and bloody, and the life of the good priest was frequently in great danger. He was, on one occasion, for many days, concealed from the hordes of savages thirsting for his blood, amidst the dense foliage of a lofty tree, and was saved only by the devotion and courage of a woman, who came at night and supplied him with food, as Grizel Baillie did her father. In the end, the Niua Foo people were all killed, and between five and six hundred of the pagan islanders took their departure, and, sailing away south, settled themselves at Vavau, one of the islands under the immediate dominion of their ancient feudal sovereign, George, king of Tonga. Since then, another internecine war took place between our friend Tunghalla and the late king. His principal stronghold was at Moa, nearly opposite the anchorage at the entrance of the reef. He had worked hard with his people, and increased much the strength of his fortifications, when, to his astonishment and intense chagrin, the people all left him to make war, under the guardianship of his gods, by himself. The missionaries' influence had increased so much, that they prevailed upon them to make peace with their neighbours, against the wishes of their chief. Since then, Tunghalla has contented himself with resting upon his laurels, and is now, he says, a Christian. But although, on the death of his old rival, he assisted in placing Lava-Lui upon the tapa, it is pretty evident that he gives her much trouble, and makes her feel that he permits her to be suzerain only because it pleases him to be a subject.

# CHAPTER XIII.

## MOA.

*24th July.*—At sunrise, this morning, we steamed down to the anchorage off Moa; and went on shore soon afterwards; Tunghalla piloted the ship from Matauto, though the Queen was desirous that he should be superseded in this privilege, and had decreed that Solomon should reign in his stead. However, as the latter, when he made his appearance on board, found the old chief at his post, he relinquished, with the best grace he could, the coveted honour, and accompanying dollars. This being the place where the oil for the fine is to be collected, and the last day for completing the quantity, we found everybody and everything redolent of the not very pleasant perfume. Men were there groaning under the weight of casks slung between poles, which they carried on their shoulders; others brought their contribution in bottles and large gourds. Poor unfortunates, from distant villages, who had been none the better for the wreck, were sitting, hungry but patient, waiting until their quota appointed by the Queen had been measured. It was a strange scene, nor was it less so, when one reflected upon the history of the place, even during the last few years. The people were now quite civil and good-humoured toward

Kitchen in Samoa.

us, all feeling that the necessity of obeying his superiors had alone compelled the Captain of the "Fawn" to trouble their peaceful waters with the presence of a war-ship. I must say I felt sorry for them, and one could not avoid feeling even ashamed, to be present, and see innocent people suffering from the misconduct of, at all events, only a few.

Some of these men pouring in their oil, were the very persons who had exerted themselves so energetically to save the lives of the countrymen of the man who, well treated by them himself for years, took advantage of his being able to make a good speculation of the loss of his vessel, by having the guns of a man-of-war brought to bear upon the houses of his hospitable entertainers.

The walk to the lake was through the usual forest scenery, varied by clearings, now and then planted with bananas, papaus, taro, etc. No sound is heard in these quiet woods, but the cooing of numbers of pigeons and doves of a beautiful plumage.

"All, save the spirit of man is divine," and now that the wars have ceased, and they worship the true God, were it not for the increasing number of white men coming to these islands, there is little doubt that the conduct and feelings of the Christianized Polynesians would be nearer perfection than those of more civilized and artificial people. The heat is certainly a great drawback to the enjoyment of any undertaking which requires exertion, but we were amply repaid for ours to-day, by the singular beauty of this old crater. It is almost perfectly circular, fine cliffs more than two hundred feet in perpendicular height render the lake almost inaccessible,—their precipitous sides being clothed most picturesquely with luxuriant hanging vegetation. In one place we found it not very difficult to descend to the edge of the deep dark water, by a path or rather staircase made by the natives, the exposed roots of the trees forming the steps. Over this hovered numbers of brilliantly white boatswain-birds; and most of the party, consisting chiefly of native boys, were soon enjoying themselves in the quiet retreat of the startled wild-ducks, the only species of water-fowl we saw, and regardless of the monstrous eels said to inhabit its depths. Our companions said that on one occasion, in another of these lakes, a man fishing from a canoe, in endeavouring to haul up his prize, was seized by the arm, dragged by the huge monster out of his boat, and narrowly escaped drowning. I saw a fisherman at Upolu, who had his hand much torn by one a few hours before, and another who had lost two of his fingers in the attempt to capture one; "like Suwarroff being taken himself instead of taking Widdin."

When we started on our walk, the chief had ordered for us an unlimited supply of cocoa-nuts, for which we thanked him in our hearts, as we sat under a shady tree, and drank that most cooling and refreshing of all liquids, the milk of the fresh young nuts, which our boys threw down and husked for us, going up to the tall trees like monkeys, with their feet tied together with a piece of the tenacious hibiscus bark.

We visited on our return the new church of Saint Joseph, not yet finished. Its dimensions are much larger, and the plan more elaborate, than those of the cathedral at Matauto. It is indeed a great undertaking, and surprisingly well executed, considering the difficulties the missionaries had to encounter in building such edifices with the limited means at their command, and by the hands of men who had never even seen a stone building, much less hewn the key-stone of an arch with chisel and mallet. The material used is a grey porphyritic stone, which is brought in well-squared blocks, smoothly chiselled, a distance of several miles by water; and the massive beams prepared for the roof are trees which grow on the hills of Fotuna one hundred and forty miles away.

No greater evidence can be produced of the influence of the missionaries, than that two priests resident here, have been able to get such laborious work perseveringly gone on with, by a people generally so averse to severe exertion.

Around the burial-ground at Moa, I observed large slabs of a coarse red porphyry, which is brought from an island in the lagoon. This is the rock of which large blocks were conveyed in former times to Tongataboo in the great war-canoes, when its chiefs or kings held this and the intermediate islands of Niua-Foo and Keppel, etc., as appanages of their kingdom. This circumstance renders more accountable the existence of the ruins of ancient buildings and circles of stones composed of materials not obtained except from distant localities, as those at Kunaie or Strong's Island, at Paasden, Easter Island, Waiahu, etc. Now all tradition of their origin is lost, and the natives regard them as the work of their godlike ancestors, who fished up the very islands themselves from the depths of the ocean.

Amongst the most singular of these remains may be mentioned those of Ascension or Ponapi, an island in lat. 7° north, and long. 157° 50′ east. They are situated upon low land, extending out upon the flats which surround the island. A writer in the Honolulu paper, the Rev. C. W. Clark, who visited them in 1852, says: "We approached the ruins from the inland side by crossing a creek or canal, from twenty to thirty feet wide, walled on both sides, and nearly dry at low tide. This led to the

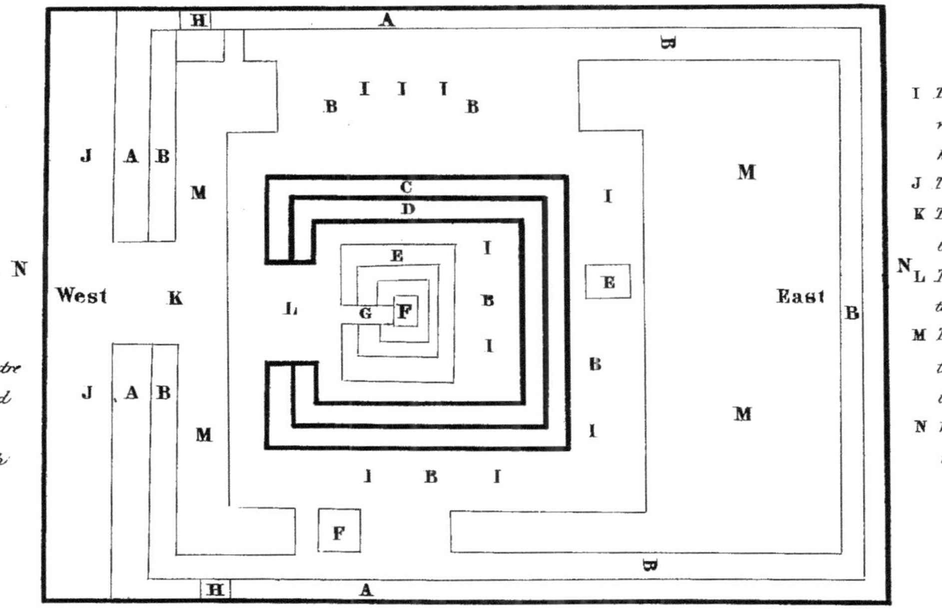


RUINS AT PUNAPET ISLAND BUILT ENTIRELY OF BASALTIC PRISMS.

SURVEYED BY M^R. CULICK.

Edmonston & Douglas, Edinburgh.

outer entrance of the ruin or fortification, which was through a large open gateway. On inspection, we found these ruins to consist of two quadrangular walls, one within the other ; the length and breadth of the outer quadrangle, by rough measurement, was 236 feet by 162 feet, and the wall from six to ten feet thick, and in some places 25 feet high on the outside. This wall seemed entire in some places, and in others, broken and overgrown with vines and trees. Proceeding a few paces from the outer wall, we came to the entrance of the inner enclosure, facing the entrance to the outer. In front of the inner is a raised platform, 10 to 12 feet wide ; the inner wall is about 14 feet high where it was not broken down, and six feet thick ; the top rows of basaltic prisms, of which the wall is built, projected over about two feet on the outside, apparently to prevent the walls from being scaled. The inner enclosure is 95 feet by 75.

"In the centre, a little raised above the surrounding ground, is a large vault. The ancient entrance to it was thoroughly closed by basaltic prisms, but I entered through a crevice in the top. The vault inside is 15 feet by 10, and 7 by 8 feet in depth. The bottom is uneven, having been dug up apparently by former visitors in search of treasure or curiosities. The top of the vault is covered with immense basaltic columns, extending the whole length, and measuring 17 feet in length. On the top, a large bread-fruit tree was growing, whose roots extended down through the vault into the ground below.

"There are several similar vaults in different parts of the ruins, between the inner and the outer walls. Human bones have been found in some of them; and small pieces of ancient coins, a silver crucifix, and a pair of silver dividers, have also, it is said, been found. These were probably left here by Spanish adventurers long before the island was generally known by the civilized world. Their origin, and the motives which prompted the builders of these ruins, are unknown to the present inhabitants."

In addition to these remains, I was informed by a credible person, whom I met in Upolu, that he had been there twelve months ago, and had seen, when sailing in his boat over the shallows, the ruins of a large town under water, with considerable buildings, regular streets, and a square in the centre, in which apparently had stood a large temple, or some such edifice.

This would militate against the idea of these

ruins having been constructed as a fortress by a colony of Spaniards, as has been supposed ; besides, it is well known by the natives that a number of people of this nation did live for some time upon this island some four or five generations ago, which sufficiently accounts for some of the discoveries made. The changes of level taking place in this part of the ocean are so great and so frequent, and the decay of buildings is so rapid in the damp hot climate, as well as the growth of trees and plants in deserted habitations, that, as in the case of the ruins of Central America, it is difficult to judge of their age from their present appearance.

In the case of these ruins, however, it is certain that the natives have no tradition whatever regarding them; and had they been the work of Spaniards, this is scarcely likely to have been the case (even after the lapse of three hundred years, the date of the occupation of the Philippines), as they are one of the finest and most intelligent races of people in these regions.

It is singular that, like the inhabitants of Ualau, Byron, and other islands of Micronesia, or Central Pacific, although living in the hottest part of the torrid zone, these people are nearly as fair as Europeans. The wives of the chiefs are quite so, seldom exposing themselves to the sun, and are celebrated for their long and beautiful hair, so different from that of their not very distant neighbours in the Kingsmill group, who are woolly-headed negroes, and very savage. Had these people been the mixed descendants of the Spaniards, some traces of the language would doubtless have remained ; but none have been observed. Their speech is harsh and discordant in sound ; and apparently more resembles that of the Chinese than of the Polynesians. Unfortunately, those interesting islanders disappear more rapidly than the darker races, in consequence of their contact with Europeans, certain terrible diseases becoming almost epidemics. Ualau, when first occupied by the American Mission, had a population of 20,000 ; last year it consisted of a miserable remnant of about 1000, or little more,—measles having lately swept away great numbers.

At Easter Island, the remains are those evidently of erections for religious purposes. They consist chiefly of broken-down terraces, with large stone statues, monuments probably of ancient deified kings, and mounds which resemble, in their triangular shape, the teocallis of Mexico. One of the statues measured by Mr. Forster was 27 feet high, and nine in diameter.

In the Marquesas also, and Sandwich Islands, there are still more extensive remains of mounds, roads, and buildings, resembling those of South America. Perhaps the American Indian and Polynesian islander, looking at the handiwork of their ancestors, have the same right to exclaim, *Ubi lapsus quid feci!*

*27th July.*—All the oil was delivered yesterday; and the cases referred to Captain Cator were settled. As usual, the chief blame, upon investigation, proved to be on the side of the white men, most of whom in these islands may safely be assumed to be rogues, unless proved to be respectable. The pilot was on board, and the anchor was about being weighed this afternoon, when a party came off from the shore to obtain redress, if possible, in a case which, as a specimen of the example set by the Europeans to the natives, may be cited:—

An elderly Portuguese brought his half-caste daughter, and showed us how she had been cut and gashed in a horrid manner by the native wife of a white trader, calling himself an American, but by his mother's side also a Portuguese, in revenge for supplanting her in her husband's affections. The girl's father admitted that he had sold her for fifty dollars, which the scoundrel-purchaser took back, after having, with some of his wife's relations, savagely beaten the miserable old man, whilst his partner, according to the custom of her race, was permitted to take her jealous *vendetta* upon the unfortunate girl in the usual manner, by cutting her with a huge jack-knife.

It is to be hoped that, both parties being amenable to punishment according to the native law, the Queen, to whom the matter had to be referred, may inflict the severest in her power. By the side of these people, on the deck, stood two respectable chiefs, one the principal executive officer of her Government. They seemed disgusted with the whole affair; and one could not but feel that the outrageous wickedness of the white men must be the greatest difficulty with which the missionaries in Polynesia have now to contend.

It is the same throughout the Pacific; and as the evil is on the increase, it were well that the Governments of civilized nations should take measures to enable the ruffians, who disgrace their respective countries, to be summarily dealt with, even unto death, by captains of ships of war visiting the various islands, when the cases have been satisfactorily proved before a court consisting of officers, and the chief missionaries and educated chiefs.

We punish severely enough any outrage committed by the natives upon our countrymen, and it is to be feared that the latter now take advantage of the terror so created to commit crimes for which the natives dare not punish them, lest their statements should be discredited, as in the case of Delaney's schooner.

Many of the massacres of crews of boats and vessels which have taken place to the westward are entirely to be attributed to the conduct of traders and masters of vessels, especially those engaged in procuring sandal-wood. It is notorious that they frequently engage the natives of an island to cut wood at places where there are few people living, or where they cannot have communication, and when the work is done land them far from home. In more than one well-authenticated instance the unfortunates have been bartered for pigs to their cannibal enemies, who, when the exchange had been made, immediately prepared their ovens in sight of the victims and the inhuman monsters who traded in their blood.

29*th July*.—After a good run of thirty hours we lay to, yesterday evening, off Horne Island, by which designation the two separate ones of Fotuna and Alofi, in lat. 14° 17′ S., and long. 178° E., are known. The former is about thirty miles in circumference, and has a population of about twelve hundred people, Alofi of three hundred, like their neighbours at Uvea, of the Tongan race.

The native pilot came off early in the morning, and took the ship under steam into the little anchorage of Singavi, where there was scarcely room for her to swing clear of the coral reefs extending out from the shore; in consequence of which the careful "Fawn" rested but a short time, and weighing anchor again, stood off and on during the day. We were soon boarded by a considerable number of natives, all wearing cotton shirts, and for the most part wrappers of the same material wreathed round the waist, with a narrow girdle of short dracæna leaves, mixed with a quantity of white flowers of a species of camomile, with a most unpleasant odour. A large proportion of them could speak English tolerably. In laying aside in great measure their native costume, they appeared also to have lost their agreeable and pleasant manners, if they ever possessed any. The gentleness and politeness, as well as the hospitality of the Samoans, were utterly wanting; and during our walk ashore the request for a cocoa-nut was replied to by the inquiry, How much tobacco would be given in exchange? The people of Tongan blood whom we have seen appear more energetic and industrious, however, than their soft-speaking neighbours; and here the extensive plantations of taro (*Arum esculentum*) at the back of the village are irrigated with much care and ingenuity. The women are certainly not good-looking, but are perhaps useful partners in their way. The beach resounded with the musical noise of the wooden mallets, with which they beat out into tissue the inner bark of the paper mulberry, first scraping it with shells, to make the siapo or native cloth, for the manufacture of which they are rather famous. Many of the men wore tall turbans of this material, uncoloured, with a fringe, which looked rather well. All profess Christianity, there being here a branch mission of the Roman Catholic Church, under the direction of the Bishop of Uvea.

The clergymen of the mission were anxious to have something done towards establishing a certain rate of pilotage for vessels coming here, and to have fixed prices for supplies, in which the titular king, who came on board, coincided with them. But the government of the island is really a republican one, and like the people with whom the most of their transactions take place, they will persist in asking as many dollars as possible for their goods, until the effect of this bad policy teaches them otherwise.

During the short time we stayed here, we saw the people of this bay only; possibly, those who have had less acquaintance with Europeans may be more pleasing in their manners. The innate pride of the Tongan race may act as a restraint upon the indulgence of curiosity; but one was struck by the display of carelessness, or else of a stupid feeling of *nil admirari* shown by the crew of a large canoe from another part of the island, carrying about thirty men, who passed by the ship, and never turned to take a second look at the English man-of-war;—not a very common object in these waters.

These islands appear of later date than the groups to the eastward, so far as their present configuration is concerned. No subsidence has taken place since their last elevation, and there is consequently no lagoon, the coral reef closely fringing the precipitous shores.

This morning, as we stood in to the land, the steam was rising from the flank of a hill in a dense column, issuing, it seemed, from a long crevice, which exposes possibly the depths of a recent field of lava to the surface waters coming down from the mountain sides. Hot springs are of very frequent occurrence in these picturesque islands. The hills, clothed half way up with dense forests, and with russet fern to the summits, reminded me of New Zealand scenery, in their rugged and furrowed outline, and their peculiar lights and shadows, particularly when seen from a distance, when the narrow cocoa-nut covered plain at their base was lost to view.

The Fotuna people indignantly denied the conquest of their island, or usurpation of the king's power, by Tungahalla, whose enterprise they said was confined to Alofi. If he and his people had ventured to land on their shore, none, they said, would have returned alive. Nevertheless, as respects the offered abdication of the chief in his favour, his possession of Alofi, and residence there for a year, at the end of which the king returned with him to Uea, his story is no doubt correct. Most probably, seeing that his authority was not likely to be much respected by the republican people of Fotuna, he thought it wiser to return to his native place.

# CHAPTER XIV.

## OFF FIJI.

1*st August.*—Since leaving Fotuna, we have glided on over the smooth waters most delightfully, though rather slowly for those anxious to receive their letters at Port de France, New Caledonia, for which place we are now steering our course. Yesterday and to-day, we have been sailing quietly over the glittering waters, just ruffled by the breath of the trade-wind, which has passed over the beautiful and fertile Fijis—the home of that strangely savage, and yet, in some respects, comparatively advanced race, of whom a very interesting description has been given by Admiral Erskine.[1] The high land of Vanua-Levu was faintly visible this morning on the soft horizon. This is all we shall see of this extensive group, upon whose shores,

[1] The intercourse between this gentleman and his officers with the natives of the various islands seems to have been conducted with great thoughtfulness and in the best spirit, and they mentioned the name of the ship, the "Havannah," with evidently pleasing recollections, in the different parts of Samoa especially.

—blest with all the choicest gifts of nature, with every advantage of beautiful scenery, balmy air, and all that can tend to soften the dispositions of man,—scenes have been daily enacted for generations probably unequalled, in savage atrocity, in the annals of the human race.[1] Yet these are people whose natural politeness and habits of decency, morality, and personal cleanliness, might be copied with advantage by civilized nations, and who display an amount of intelligence, energy, and industry much greater than that met with amongst the majority of the gentler and more attractive Polynesians.

On the cold and inhospitable shores of Tierra del Fuego, when the long-protracted winter has reduced the miserable, shivering savages to the brink of starvation, the old women crawl tremblingly away from the family camp, and hide in some lonely cave, where they subsist upon raw shell-fish, until their footsteps are tracked, and they are brought back by their relatives, to be smothered in the smoke of their own hearths. It is considered expedient to sacrifice them rather than the dogs, because, as they say, "Doggies catch otters; old women no."[2] Under the shade of the beautiful cocoa-nut and

[1] See Appendix, No. III.

[2] *Voyage of the "Beagle."*

bread-fruit trees, where no such dire necessity arises to deaden the instinctive feelings of nature, parents are treated with great barbarity. When age and its failings begin to tell upon the Fiji chief, his son digs his grave, and, telling his father that his time is come, leads him forth to it, fanning him by the way, and then, laying him down alive upon the bodies of his strangled wives, hastily covers him over with earth, amidst songs and savage chants, which drown his groans.

We are now again in the eastern hemisphere, in the parallel of 178° west longitude, which passes between the Tonga and Fiji groups, dividing that part of Polynesia tenanted by the dark and crisp-haired Papuans, from the region of the light copper-coloured and straight-haired race. This line, however, does not include New Zealand, inhabited by people of the same blood, whose ancestors seem most probably to have come from Savaii. "The seed of our coming," say the Maories, "is from Hawaiki, the seed of food, the seed of men."[1] *Hawaiki* being the form of the word Savaii in their dialect, in which, as in the Tongan and others, the *s* is changed to *h*, and *k* is frequently inserted before a vowel at the end of a word. Another tradi-

[1] Sir George Grey's *Traditions of New Zealand*, Appendix.

tion is, that near Hawaiki, their ancestral home, lay the islands of Waerota, Waeroto, Rarotonga, Parima, and Manono. The Rarotongans also claim Savaii (or Hawaiki as they also call it) as the abode of their forefathers; whilst Apolima and Manono were likely to be well remembered, exercising as they did, from time immemorial, much influence on the adjacent larger islands, as the head-quarters of the "Malo." There is a curious fact mentioned by Mr. Williams, in his missionary tour, that, when he first visited the New Zealanders, he found them in possession of a domestic dog, identical in appearance with that found wild at Manono. The two other islands mentioned may have been small ones which have perhaps since then disappeared during some of the periods of great disturbance which have occurred from time to time. In one of these, so lately as 1846, an island between the Samoan and Friendly group, was reduced from the condition of a beautiful, fertile, and populous little land, to a mass of cinders and ashes.

I was struck one day at Apia by the strong resemblance between a Maori and Rarotongan, two men belonging to a boat's crew; the latter having the high nose of the New Zealander, probably from not being flattened in infancy, as is the custom in

Samoa, where "a canoe nose," as it is termed, is considered a great blemish.

The lesser Hawaiki, sometimes spoken of by the New Zealanders, where their ancestors remained for some generations, is, in all probability, Rarotonga, there having been much intercourse in former times between the people of the Hervey and Samoan groups.

The physical strength of the broad-shouldered Maori is partly owing, no doubt, to the difference of climate and food; but it seems not at all unlikely that one source of the great variety of features observable amongst them is an admixture, subsequent to their first leaving Savaii, perhaps whilst at Rarotonga, of other blood in their veins, Japanese perhaps, and mingled with it an infusion of that of some North American Indian race, originally themselves, probably, springing from the same branch of the Asiatic family as the Dyaks of Borneo, the Bugis of the Celebes, and the Polynesians. This supposition is strengthened by the existence of many analogous customs, and by a curious circumstance mentioned by the Rev. Mr. Taylor in his work on New Zealand. He states that some years ago a party of Maories were observed with a singular-looking bell in their possession, which was used as a cooking utensil, and on examination, was found by the missionaries to have Japanese characters engraved upon it. It was discovered, they said, long ago, under the root of an old tree blown down near the shore. The peculiar high nose of the North American Indians may have been inherited from some mixed descendants of the two races. In 1830, a large Japanese junk was wrecked upon the coast of Vancouver Island, and in 1836, another on one of the Sandwich Islands, and the crews settled at these places. Similar accidents have no doubt frequently occurred amongst these maritime people; and the involuntary emigrants, with their wives and children, or their descendants, may have again put to sea, and reached some of the islands of Polynesia. Very possibly, too, the Samoan and Hervey Islanders had received a dash of Mongolian blood into their veins from the islands of Micronesia. The Chinese always have been great wanderers, as were the Japanese previous to 1637. The former have strongly marked their character and features upon many of the inhabitants of the islands of northern and central Pacific; and Captain Sherard Osborne and others have remarked the resemblance in the physiognomy and soft-sounding language of the

Japanese to the true Polynesians. The traditions of the people of Tonga, the Society, Marquesas, and other islands, also point to Samoa as their birth-place, that group having been no doubt the resting-place of the ancient Malayan or Tagalic colony, from which the different islands have been peopled by their descendants; whilst New Guinea seems to have been the headquarters of the Papuan or Melanesian. Between them an infinite number of varieties have sprung up, observable in the features, complexion, and language, in almost every group of islands, in some still more or less complicated by the alliance with the Micronesians, under which designation the people of the Pelew Isles, Carolines, Mariana, Tarawa, etc. are comprehended. The love of migration is still strong among the so-called Malayo-Polynesians, especially the inhabitants of smaller islands, such as Newe, Fotuna, Uea, etc., where the people, even the women, beseech captains of ships to give them passages to unknown countries. This feeling, together with involuntary emigration in canoes driven off shore being taken into account, renders it not difficult to explain the changes that have taken place, and which are still going on, in the features and customs of the different islanders.

A few months ago a whale-ship picked up off Tokilau,[1] one of the Union group, a large canoe full of people of both sexes of the negro race, whose language was quite unintelligible to a Rotumah man on board. No doubt they had been driven out to sea by an unexpected *vale* (a mad or foolish wind), as the Samoans call the north-westers, from the Kingsmill or Gilbert Islands, where they were landed, the ship happening to be bound in that direction. Had they reached Fakaa-fo, the inhabitants being of a kindly disposition, would probably have received them hospitably, and a change would have been effected similar to that referred to at Matauto in Savaii, which has been brought about by the Fijian colonists.

It is natural to imagine that (as in the case of the Polynesians) a people whose language is poor will gladly avail themselves of a new name for an object, their own word for which, was one having many other meanings. Thus in Samoa the syllable *Na*, besides being a particle marking the imperfect tense, standing for the pronouns *he*, *she*, *this*, *that*, or *those*, is also used as a verb signifying to hush, to quiet a child, to conceal, to deny; and *Aa* may

[1] See Appendix, No. IV.

mean the fibres of a root, family connexion; or with the addition of the breath or slight aspirate, the husk of a cocoa-nut, a species of fish, and an exclamation of disappointment. Many English words have been adopted into the Samoan tongue, and, with a modification, are in common use.

Another mode in which a change takes place in the dialect, or language rather, of tribes living in the same island, is in consequence of words being tabooed from use. Thus when a chief happens to bear the name of some familiar object, a new one must be invented for that object, as the word must no longer be desecrated by being applied to any less worthy purpose. At Pago-Pago it would have been the height of indecorum to have used the word *mauga,* a hill or mountain, in the Samoan, Tahitian, Tongan, and New Zealand dialects, when speaking to the chief of the wooded peak of Matafoa which rises opposite his dwelling, his family having assumed that designation.

In these and other ways the language of the people of the same race, living even in a small island, often becomes so distinct as to be unintelligible to one another. This is the case at Tanna, where constant wars have kept the people of the northern and southern portions of the island apart for generations, and also amongst the equally unsettled tribes of New Caledonia. To the same cause, on a greater scale, amongst the North American Indians, is to be attributed the existence of about 400 languages or idioms, as stated by Balbi, and about 4000 dialects.

I was told by an intelligent French missionary who had been amongst the Indians of the Zûnis and other tribes of Western North America, that he could trace a resemblance between many of their words and the Tongan.

Mr. Hale and other philologists may yet arrive at conclusions from further acquaintance with the various idioms, which will afford more satisfactory proofs of the relationship existing between the descendants of the Barrow-raising Scythians of North America, the Japanese, and the Polynesians; and possibly some evidence may yet be obtained to show that there is reason to believe that the woolly-headed Tasmanian, the remnant of the aborigines of New Zealand, said still to exist on the west coast of the middle island, the savages of the Andaman Islands, and those of the mountains of Borneo and Java, may be the scattered descendants of a race that inhabited part of the great central continent, the fabled Lanka of the Brahmins, the blood of some of whose prehistoric races still runs strong in the veins of the Melanesians.

We are aware that the present arrangement of land and sea is far different from that of ancient days. So frequent and great have been the changes, that the different aspects of the surface of the globe are beyond the power of our imagination to picture, during the various long epochs that have passed since the comparatively late geological era, when the Pterodactyle winged its solemn flight over the land and sea tenanted by the giant saurians; and we are equally unable to conceive what scenes will be displayed hereafter, for the forces which have effected those changes still give evidence of their ability to produce convulsions as great; and we see preparations going quietly and steadily on for the reproduction of many of the most imposing features of the present continents perhaps on a grander scale. One can well conceive that the scenery which will be displayed to the view of the future inhabitant of the continent, which will perhaps again lie fair to the tropical sun, where the blue Pacific now washes the shores of countless islands, will in grandeur and beauty far surpass any of the present lands.

Geologists now generally entertain the idea first

broached by that eminent geologist, Professor Ansted, that the Himalayas existed as a chain of islands, and were elevated into their present lofty position by the same convulsions that raised up the steppes of Siberia, Tartary, and a great part of Europe, and submerged the great continent of the torrid zone, whose previous existence is marked by the Lacadives, Maldives, the Chagos group and the coral islands in the Indian Ocean, and possibly connected Sumatra and other islands of the Indian Archipelago with the Malay peninsula.

The great affinity existing between the language of the people of Madagascar and the Tagals of the Philippines, mentioned by old Spanish authors, is a curious circumstance bearing upon this hypothesis. The Atolls of the Pacific afford unmistakable evidence of what has taken place to the eastward, and perhaps at a comparatively recent date the stepping stones from the Indian to the Polynesian islands may have been more numerous than now, as well as those between the shores of Arabia and the Eastern Archipelago.

On the whole, it seems probable that the tide of emigration which originally set from east to west divided into two streams, one of which may have passed, by way of the Aleutian Islands, to

America, from the intertropical shores of which continent the current flowed back again fitfully, in after times, to the westward.

The emigrants, wafted on by the south-east trade-wind, came from time to time, perhaps, to the different islands of the Pacific, some of which they found peopled by the descendants of men of the same original type, who had passed to Oceania from the peninsulas of southern Asia, whilst others may have landed upon the shores of those inhabited by the progeny of an older but inferior race of colonists of a totally different type, flat-featured and woolly-headed, whose standard they, to a certain extent, served to elevate, as in the case of the Fijians.

From whatever source the negro population came to those seas, it is clear that they must have resided in their insulated abodes for a long time, and the conclusion is almost forced upon us, that latitude is not the cause of difference of colour in the human race. In Tasmania, in lat. 45°, the woolly-headed aborigines were black as the Nubian; whilst we find many of the natives of the islands of the central part of the torrid zone fair as the people of southern Europe. If the change be effected by the influence of climate, an immense lapse of time must be granted, and the supporters of the proposition must be prepared to admit that the gradual change had been accomplished in ages gone by, before the negro slaves were brought from the plains of Ethiopia by the Egyptian Pharaohs.

If such be the case, the existence of man contemporaneously with some of the extinct great animals need not be considered improbable.

*6th August.*—The light trade wind and fine weather, which, after our unusually bad luck in experiencing so much wet, have carried us past the New Hebrides and Loyalty Islands, failed us on the 4th in lat. 20° 35′, and long. 171° E., where we were met by a sudden squall from the south-west, which reduced the temperature ten degrees in a few minutes. The thermometer stood at 69°, which we felt a most agreeable change from 80° in the cabin, below which the mercury has not fallen for two months, and slightly compensated us for the constant rain which followed for thirty hours. We are now eighty miles from Aneitum, in which island the clergy of the London Mission have accomplished much. A stone church has been built by the natives, who but a few years ago were addicted to all the most savage practices. In no island was the custom of strangling wives on the death of their husbands carried to a greater extent; and even mothers on the death of a favourite child went with it to the "land of spirits." Their souls took their departure for Umatmas (as it is called) by jumping from a rock on the western extremity of that island, as the Samoans think theirs do from the west end of Savaii. So infatuated are these people in the various parts of Melanesia where the custom prevails, that on several occasions, when attempts have been made to save the lives of the victims of superstition, they themselves have indignantly insisted upon their right to accompany the departed, and have in some cases strangled themselves.

We regret this unpropitious weather the more, as it shuts out from us a possible glimpse of Tanna, with its grand volcano.

This island, which is densely peopled for its size, the number of its negro aborigines being estimated at from eighteen to twenty thousand, was the scene of the sufferings and dangers undergone by the brave missionaries, Mr. Pratt and Mr. Turner. The latter has written an entertaining work on these islands, which was given me by one of his associates, and which we should have been glad to have possessed sooner on the voyage.

The people of Tanna have suffered much of late

years from European diseases, as they had done at the time those gentlemen had to fly for their lives; and the priests of the mountain have made the most of the opportunity to embitter the feelings of the people against the disease-bringing teachers of the new religion, and white men in general. These feelings have not been improved much by the affrays which have taken place with the traders in search of sandal-wood and sulphur. Not very long ago, Captain Grant had a very narrow escape here. Cruising for whales in the neighbourhood, and falling short of water, he stood in along the coast, and observing a little bay where solitude seemed to reign, no smoke or signs of life being visible, pulled in a whale-boat with some casks to the shore, in hopes of finding a stream coming down from the mountain. Just as they reached the beach, a tremendous shout arose from the jungle, and down rushed some hundred painted savages, who seized the boat, and dragged it up high and dry amongst the mangroves, with the crew sitting in their places. Death seemed almost inevitable. Grant thought, at all events, the most prudent course was not to irritate them by any useless attempt at resistance against such overwhelming odds, and made his men sit still in the boat. After a long and stormy debate amongst their captors, of whom it appeared some were taking their part, by the different gesticulations of the speakers, as they pointed to their prisoners, to their infinite relief and astonishment, their friends proved successful, and the crowd taking their boat as before, bore them back into the water, motioning to them to be off, a hint they gladly took, and plied their oars, no doubt, with good-will, as they returned to the ship thirsty as they came. Standing round to the other side of the island, where there were a number of Europeans getting sandal-wood, they found they had still more reason to congratulate themselves upon their lucky escape, and the forbearance of the natives, when they learned from them that, a few weeks ago, a number of the people of that very bay had been shot by the white men.

At a few hours' sail from Tanna lies Erromango, where the memorable tragedy was enacted in 1839; when the good old Mr. Williams and Mr. Harris, another missionary, met their deaths. Subsequent events have added to the terrible interest of the locality. The Rev. Mr. Gordon took up his residence, and built a church there. But he and his wife have lately met a similar fate, under circumstances of great treachery, and been added to the numerous list of martyrs in the cause of converting the savages of the New Hebrides. Report states that he had imprudently, in urging the natives to abandon some heathen atrocity, said that the possible vengeance of Heaven might fall on them, if they persisted in disregarding his warnings, and that they might be swept off by pestilence. Believing as these people do, that their own priests, and, of course, in a much greater degree, the missionaries, have power to cause or to avert such visitations, no doubt they immediately adopted the surest way, as they thought, to prevent such a catastrophe, by killing those likely to bring it upon them. The missionaries themselves, deeply as they feel for the miserable fate of their companions, are not advocates for the punishment of these people. Savages they are doubtless in the fullest acceptation of the word, but what have they learned from the practices of the white men to make them ashamed of their cruelties? Except from the missionaries themselves, whose precepts and example are derided, it is to be feared, that from the majority of the pale-faces who have come amongst them, they have learned more of evil than of good. These islands of the New Hebrides, especially, have been the scenes of atrocities committed by them, quite equalling, and almost excelling in barbarity and treachery those of the cannibal natives themselves; and about four hundred persons engaged in the trade have lost their lives in Erromango and Tanna alone, since the sandal-wood was discovered there, in consequence of the diabolical acts of some.

The people of these two islands are deadly enemies; and the traders are in the habit of engaging men from the former to cut the wood, taking them to the enemies' country, and having got their work done, then leaving them to their certain fate, saying, when asked where they are on their return, "Oh, they were killed in Erromango at a fight," or *vice versa*, when they have gone from Erromango to Tanna. So many Tanna men have been killed in this way at Erromango, that an Erromangan cannot expect, Mr. Turner says, to live five minutes after landing anywhere on the Tannese coast.

Dogs and cats are in great demand at Erromango, and are to be had at Tanna. Mr. Turner saw with his own eyes a quantity of these animals brought on board a schooner at the latter place, from which an Erromango man had been landed and killed that morning; and naturally could not divest his mind of the conviction that the unfortunate being who immediately formed the means of a repast to his captors, had been given in payment for them. It is almost incredible that in these times such deeds should be perpetrated by men sailing under the flag of England, and who escape the punishment due to their crimes from the arm of the law, although a dire retribution often falls upon them from the hands of the natives. No wonder that instead of regarding them any longer as sailing gods, they have designated the people that visit their shores in sandal-wood ships, sailing profligates or devils.

11*th August.*—We have been fighting our way for the last few days against what we may well call a hard-hearted wind; for it has blown right in our teeth, neither permitting us to steer our proper course, nor to go into the harbour of the islands, which we have tantalizingly seen in the distance. On the 8th we sighted Aneitum, which rises to the height of 2500; and on the 9th, the wind veering from SW. to NW., carried us on our way for some hours at the rate of nine knots. We congratulated ourselves on the probability of being at anchor on the following day, when suddenly, half an hour after ten knots had been logged, the "Fawn" was provokingly fanning herself after her exertions, with her sails idly flapping in a calm. It was not, however, of long duration, for a strong south-wester soon came up, reducing the thermometer to 65°, the barometer standing at 29° 80′. Against this we have been tacking backwards and forwards between the islands of Nengone, the most southern of the Loyalties, and the Isle of Pines.

Yesterday we were quite close to the former (Mare, as it is called in the charts), an uplifted mass of coral which presents the appearance of two distinct elevations. Its height is about 250 feet. Groups of remarkable columnar-looking pine-trees (*Araucaria Cookii*) give, as in the other islands in this part of the Pacific, a most peculiar aspect to the scenery. The population numbers about 10,000 of the dark race, who have made themselves notorious in the history of these seas, like many of their neighbours, not only by their revolting customs, but by their successful attacks upon trading vessels.

Now, thanks to the exertions of the London Mission clergymen, half of them profess Christianity. Against them, as a consequence, fierce war is now waged by the heathen tribes in the eastern part of the island. The labours of the individual missionaries here are deserving of the highest praise and appreciation ; and the energy with which they conduct the operations of the Society is sufficiently testified by the fact, that on this savage island, a printing-press is now at work, and large portions of the Bible have been translated into the language of Nengone and of Uea. The latter island is also being civilized under the auspices of the Society, and of that most noble and energetic Englishman, Bishop Selwyn, justly called the apostle of the Pacific, who has done so much for the conversion of the inhabitants of the islands of this part of the ocean, and those lying farther north. He has himself made more than one adventurous voyage amongst them from New Zealand, steering his little craft of twenty tons' burden with his own hands, and escaping death on more than one occasion only by the awe inspired for the moment by his striking presence and manly bearing.

His mantle has fallen on his successor, Bishop Pattison, who is now metropolitan of the diocese of Oceania, and whose enthusiasm in the cause and adventurous intrepidity almost equal his own.

## CHAPTER XV.

### KUNAIE, OR THE ISLE OF PINES.

12*th August.*—Yesterday evening we stood close to the shore of Kunaie, or the Isle of Pines, which name has been pretty generally adopted by the aborigines, who speak of their country as Ileopin. They have been conspicuous even amongst the savage races of these western islands by their great bravery, physical superiority, and most superlative barbarity. A change has now come over the scene in every way, and their energies are more devoted to the cultivation of their grounds, in which their superiority over their neighbours in New Caledonia is as much manifested as it formerly was in war.

The wind falling lighter, the "Fawn" did not go into the anchorage, but stood off, and beat up during the night along the reef, which encloses both, to the entrance through it to the north, off the southern point of New Caledonia. We steamed in through the passage to-day, in a lovely calm morning, skirting the shores for forty miles, and anchored in the snug harbour of Port de France at two P.M. The coast, at a little distance, in its colour and configuration, resembles that of the Red Sea, being generally equally barren.

At the entrance of a narrow channel, called Woodin Canal, however, the scenery is peculiar and striking. High, bare, red hills slope abruptly down

The Isle of Pines.

to the shore. In the sheltered recesses of the numerous little bays, a few cocoa-nuts growing around the conical huts of the natives, alone testified that we had not yet crossed the tropic, whilst above, those strange Araucarias truly cast anchor in the rifted rock. Of all the natural curiosities of this part of the world, none struck me so much as those unique vegetable productions. One can easily imagine, when seen for the first time, their being mistaken by the early navigators of those seas, for columns, masts of ships, towers, or even "*pillars of basaltes, like to those which compose the Giant's Causeway in Ireland*," as Captain Cook says "*his philosophers were positive they were.*"

Standing by itself on a rocky pinnacle, we saw one which was especially difficult to imagine to be a veritable growing tree. The peculiarity of their appearance is given by the branches growing thickly out round the trunk, from the root to the top of the tree, being all of the same length, except the younger fronds at the very summit, which, in many specimens, rather project, like the capital of some stately column.

Emerging from the contracted channel, we passed close by a rocky islet, well named the Porc-épic, for the sea porcupine, abounding in these waters, does not bristle more with spines than it does with its tall pine-trees, on the eastern sides chiefly, for they seem to require the moist breath of the trade-wind, the western slopes of the hills and islands being generally destitute of timber.

A few years ago, this rather sterile shore resounded only with the war-cries and booming lalis of its wild aborigines. To-day the bugles rang out shrilly in the calm bright air, as we landed on the Quai Napoléon, and passed up the Rue Magenta, enlivened with the uniforms of artillery-men, Zouaves, gendarmes, etc., to call upon his Excellency Governor Guillain, lately arrived to take charge of the affairs of the colony.

The town has prospered well during the six years which have elapsed since the occupation of this large island by the French. It is very neat and clean, and well laid out; but whether it will ever be a populous one is very doubtful. The temptations to emigrate to New Caledonia are not by any means great, and the number of civilians here is much less than it was three years ago. The climate is, no doubt, very salubrious, but the amount of good land is limited. At present there is no exportable article produced, except a small quantity of cocoa-nut oil, in the more northern portion of the island, the settlement being entirely supported by the large Government expenditure. It is a sort of penal establishment at present; soldiers and conscripts who have committed more venial crimes are sent here for the period they would have had to serve as regulars, and under the cognomen of *disciplinaires*, are employed in making roads and other public works, being at the same time under strict military discipline. The system seems to work well, and the greatest order is apparent everywhere.

In this way the colony is useful, and possibly may prove valuable by and by, in other respects. The bay of Port de France is surrounded by hills rising tier above tier, as they recede towards the main range forming the back-bone of the island, which, being chiefly composed of serpentine, breaking through argillaceous and micaceous schists and slates, apparently of Silurian age, is rugged and barren in the extreme. The lower country is covered with coarse grass, and in parts lightly timbered with the desolate-looking *Melaleuca leucodendron*, with its uncomfortable, tattered bark (similar to that of the Australian species of the tea-tree, as the colonists call it), and white stems often charred with fire, like the stunted white gum-trees on an Australian hill, and with the casuarina, the "wizard she-oak," as Bulwer calls it.

On the whole, the landscape is even less tropical looking than the generality of the Australian coast in the same latitude, which, however, it resembles a good deal in many ways. Clouds of large grasshoppers to-day drifted before the breeze, like snow-flakes in the sun. Their numbers are fortunately diminished lately. A few weeks ago the labours of the settlers were of little avail, every green thing being speedily devoured by them. This visitation, people say, occurs about every third season. Numbers of large brown kites followed in their wake, sometimes turning aside to chase the small brown quail, startled by some passing naked aboriginal, as on the adjacent continent.

Coming from the rich vegetation of the luxuriant islands of the north, the impression given by a first view of this part of New Caledonia is not favourable. The "enchantment lent by distance to the view" is gone completely on nearer inspection, as amongst the brown hills of New Zealand.

13*th August.*—I rode out to-day to the mission of La Conception, eight miles from the port. The well-made road runs for a considerable distance through an undulating country. Some of the views are pretty, and there is always in sight the fine mountain range; but there is a bleakness and uninviting look in the landscape, which must be the case when the inhospitable-looking melaleuca is the prevailing tree. In the valleys the soil is good, and the bananas, cotton plants, yams, and taro seemed very flourishing in the well-cultivated grounds of the mission, where coffee and sugarcanes also thrive well alongside pease, potatoes, and other vegetables.

We were hospitably received by P. P. Rougeyron, the Superior of the Marist Fathers, who seemed to have much on his hands to attend to, having more than a hundred scholars to lead, as well as the direction of the temporal affairs of the extensive establishment, and to-day he was engaged in the particular services of the Church, this being the festival of St. Napoleon. The missionaries have chosen for themselves here a commanding situation, looking towards the eastern waters. In front is the picturesque little island of Porc-épic, and to the left Mont d'Or rises abruptly to the height of four thousand three hundred feet. The consolation of a cheerful prospect in the distance, encouraging them to look forward to better times, must have been much required here in former years, for the country all round is in its natural state, as destitute of interest and attraction, as its inhabitants are unpleasing in appearance and repulsive in manners and habits. There is now a considerable native village around the mission settlement, and success is at last attending the efforts made to civilize the New Caledonians, which seemed at one time an almost hopeless task, the mission having been abandoned at one time in consequence of the hostility of the savages. We saw a considerable number of those people of the Negrillo race to-day. Many of the men are active, well-made fellows, with crisp rather than woolly hair rather tufted, projecting lips, retreating narrow foreheads, and noses artificially flattened. Most have the lobes of their ears pierced and distended to an immense extent, with pieces of wood gradually increased in size until the orifice has attained fashionable dimensions. Clothes are generally dispensed with, when they are not obliged to wear them at the mission, and in the principal street of Port de France. Even there I saw many exquisites in a full costume of rather a meagre description. It consists of a turban of scarlet cloth, if possible, if not, of white, with a plume of feathers; a little string with a knot at the end of it, made of the fur of the Rousette, tied round the first finger of the right hand, used in throwing their spears, one of which they generally carry; and one other article of dress, impossible to describe, which our ideas of propriety would certainly induce us to recommend their dispensing with altogether. "Les dieux n'ont fait que deux choses parfaites, la femme et la rose." To our undiscriminating eyes, little of that perfection has been inherited by the women of New Caledonia, who, notwithstanding, appear to consider that beauty when unadorned is adorned the most, and content themselves with a fringe, three or four inches deep, round the loins. They are much more degraded than the generality of South Sea Islanders, and are compelled to a life of drudgery. Polygamy obtains to a great extent. In proportion to the number of a chief's harem, so is the abundance of his yams and taro. So little value is placed on the lives of females, that Buaret, a well-known chief in the north, used to practise with a musket at a row of unfortunate creatures set up as targets, whom he ruthlessly shot down one by one.

They have few attractions, with the exception of tolerable figures; the anxiety to preserve their symmetry being the chief cause of infanticide, which is very common. The men have beards, but seldom permit them to grow; whiskers are, however, considered ornamental, and a man without them is deemed to be cursed by the gods. For generations war has been the daily business of the New Caledonians, who are so divided in consequence, that they have not even a name for the whole island. Children make their entry into the world always in the door-way of the house, and are nearly white when born. On such occasions all the friends and neighbours are assembled around. If the infant be a boy, it is at once consecrated to the god of war, and a certain black stone, brought from Lifu, is used on the occasion, that his heart may be strong and hardy in battle. If a girl, she is betrothed to one of the bystanders, perhaps to her own brother; for, as in the matter of dress, they resemble the Andaman Islanders also in their perfect disregard of consanguinity. The first lesson taught a child is to fight with its companions. Keenness of sight and quickness of hearing being qualities of the utmost importance, are sought to be increased by practice from earliest youth. Like the aborigines of Australia, they lay themselves down on the ground, and listen for the steps of the approaching foe, which they can distinguish at a great distance. Women accompany their husbands and brothers to battle, not to assist them in the fight, but to drag away the fallen adversaries, and prepare their bodies for the banquet, serving them up often entire, cooked in a sitting posture, painted and arrayed in war costume. Imagination revolts from such scenes, which still take place in undiminished atrocity in some parts of the island. Their priests encouraged fighting as much as lay in their power; the hands of the enemy were their portion ; and if the number to which they considered themselves entitled at certain intervals were not forthcoming, threats of disease quickly aroused the superstitious people to renew the attacks upon their neighbours. Those that fall of the victorious party are brought home with loud lamentations, and buried with great wailing and shrieking from the appointed mourners, who remain unclean often for several years, after burying a great chief, and are subject to many strict observances. For weeks they continue nightly to waken the forest echoes with their cries. After ten days have elapsed the grave is opened, and the head twisted off; and again, in this custom resembling the Andaman Islanders, the teeth are distributed as relics amongst the relatives, and the skull preserved as a memento by the nearest of kin, who daily goes through the form of offering it food. The only exceptions are in the case of the remains of old women, whose teeth are sown in the yam patches as a charm to produce good crops; their skulls set up upon poles being deemed equally potent in this respect.

There is reason to believe that these people have retrograded considerably, and that at one time, since their settlement in New Caledonia, they were in a much more advanced state. Remains of ancient aqueducts are to be seen, one eight miles in length; also of paved roads and fortifications. "We are not," they say, "like our ancestors; we cannot build large houses as they did; they were numerous and wise, we are neither one nor the other." The learned P. P. Montrouzier, one of the mission clergymen, found that there exists among them a singular custom, resembling that described by MM. Huc and Gabet in their interesting journal of travels in Thibet and Tartary. When a stranger arrives, the first ceremony on his reception is exchanging a little white or red scarf. When two friends meet, they exchange the scarf of good luck called Ava or Uangi at Balado, Titi at Yengen, *Kata* at Kanatoa, and along the south coast. M. Huc describes the Khata, or scarf of felicity, as a prominent feature in Thibetan manners. This is his account of it:—"The Khata, then, is a piece of silk nearly as fine as gauze, and of so very pale a blue as to be almost white. There are khatas of all sizes and all prices, for a khata is an object with which neither poor nor rich can dispense. No one ever moves unless provided with a supply. When you go to pay a visit, to ask a favour, or to acknowledge one, you begin with displaying the khata. You take it in both hands, and offer it to the person you desire to honour. When two friends meet, their first proceeding is to exchange a khata; it is as much a matter of course as shaking hands is in Europe. One cannot exaggerate the importance which the Thibetans, the Si-fan, the Houng-ma-Eul, and all the people who dwell towards the western shores of the Blue Sea, attach to the ceremony of the khata. The most gracious words, the most magnificent presents, go for nothing if unaccompanied by the khata." The taboo obtains amongst the New Caledonian aborigines, as amongst the Polynesians and most of the Papuan races. So also does circumcision, or rather concision, and the language of ceremony addressed to the chiefs.

The total population at present is estimated at from 18,000 to 20,000; and as the natural productions of the country are not so rich and abundant as those of the islands to the east and north, they are compelled to devote more labour and attention to their yam and taro grounds. They use tools made of serpentine, which also serves for the axes with which they shape their canoes, after being first hollowed by fire. The canoes resemble in form those of the Samoans, but are of much inferior workmanship. The only manufacture in which they (like their near relatives, the Fijians) have advanced beyond the Polynesians, is that of a coarse pottery made by the women from the Kaolin clay, which is abundant. They varnish it with the gum of the dammara, and paint it with red ochre. With this also they ornament their houses, which are thatched close down to the ground, and made almost air-tight. In these they sit, half stifled in heat and smoke, and come out naked into the sharp winds that blow in winter from the south. To this cause, no doubt, are to be attributed the diseases of the lungs from which many of them die. Though stoutly built, they are a short-lived race, few reaching the age of sixty, so far as the missionaries have been able to ascertain.

Their country is certainly not very inviting, and its natural history does not possess any great novelty. Of mammalia, with the exception of the rousettes and mice, there are none indigenous. There is no large struthious bird; but pigeons, one species of which makes the woods resound with its loud but melancholy cooing, doves, quail, wild ducks, and paroquets are common; also a beautiful little species of sparrow. To these are to be added, as making up the ornithological catalogue, one species of owl, the sparrow-hawk, two species of crows, the buzzard, the heron, one or two small birds, and a fine handsome *megapode*, with lilac plumage and crest, called Radyou by the natives. This bird is much sought after as a delicacy for the tables of the French gourmands. Like other nearly wingless birds elsewhere, it is consequently becoming very rare, and I could not obtain a specimen.

The sea compensates the people of New Caledonia for the poverty of the land productions. Fish are abundant, and very fine. At certain seasons, however, many species become very unwholesome, especially a sardine and a diodon, called Mambo by the natives, by which several people were poisoned lately at Port de France. The Dugong is also an occasional visitor of these shores, and is as much prized as by the aborigines of Australia. Land serpents are unknown, but three species of water snakes are common. They are viviparous, and possess a double row of teeth, but are harmless.

It has been supposed by some geologists, that New Caledonia and the New Hebrides were at one time connected with Australia; but the fauna and flora are so different that this does not seem to have been the case, unless at a very remote geological epoch. The marsupials of Australia are unrepresented in New Caledonia, in which large island not one of the snakes common to that continent is found. Nor are alligators known in its rivers, whilst in the islands of Torres Straits, the Solomon group, New Guinea, New Britain, and New Ireland, and even in Woodlark Island, both snakes and alligators are common, as well as the phalanger and flying squirrel; whilst the numerous families of the Proteaceæ and Epacridaceæ of Australia are also only represented by one or two individuals.[1]

18*th August.*—We weighed anchor this morning, and made sail for Norfolk Island, having spent the week very pleasantly among the agreeable resi-denters in this remote and rather out-of-the-way French colony, who seemed to enjoy our visit as a relief to the monotony of their lives. We were entertained with parties at Government House and elsewhere, French dinners, little dances, and other amusements, in the country of the wild New Caledonians.

Saturday was to have been our day for sailing, but Captain Cator complied with the particular request of the Governor that he would remain and witness the "grand fête," which took place yesterday, Sunday, in honour of his Imperial Majesty's birthday.

[1] Sir Emerson Tenent mentions that the fauna and flora of Ceylon resemble those of Australia more than of India.

Since our arrival, the population of the settlement has received a considerable accession, the frigate "Isis" having come in on Friday, fitted up as a store-ship, bringing about three hundred emigrants, and a large supply of goods from France: amongst other things, I observed large quantities of planks stowed in her chains, good timber not being procurable nearer than New Zealand or Queensland, a want which will be felt by the settlers.

A schooner, belonging to the Government, also returned during the week, from a cruise round the island, bringing a large number of native chiefs to witness the festivities; the greater number of them walking about the town in their eccentric attire.

Sunday morning was ushered in by the sound of martial music. The ships were all gaily dressed by sunrise, and never was there in so young a colony, so precocious a display of uniforms, and military pomp and circumstance. There were reviews, marchings, bugles sounding, drums beating, flags flying in every direction; a very fair regatta, native games and dances, amusements of various kinds, *cochons* with greasy tails, and so on; and in the evening a very creditable display of fireworks was made at the artillery barracks. Every one seemed to forget La Belle France for the day, and determined to enjoy himself. H.M.S. "Fawn" added not a little to the gay appearance of the harbour, and her salute made the echoes wake far up the mountain sides. The natives appeared in high good humour; and three friendly chiefs, with beards and moustache *à l'Empereur*, received gold medals and crimson scarfs from the Governor, of which they were not a little proud.

The impression the lively scene must have given of their new home to the late arrivals will not, it is to be hoped, be found by them to be altogether too favourable. The *Moniteur* of the Port de France speaks of the Governor as the "legitimate hope of better things for New Caledonia." There is no doubt, that under his active and energetic supervision, and the direction of the very able engineers in charge, the public works will go on with vigour. But his difficulty will be to induce the settlers to undertake the systematic production of some staple article of export.

At one time, the valleys of New Caledonia were reported to be rich in the precious metals. The geological formation is analogous to that of Australia to a certain extent, and gold no doubt exists, but in limited quantities probably, the auriferous formations not being largely developed, so far as I can ascertain. Iron is abundant, and copper has also been found, as well as coal; but the only deposit of the latter hitherto discovered is of very limited extent, being apparently in a small isolated basin, of the same age as the coal of the middle island of New Zealand.

The expectation that it would be an important wool-producing country does not seem likely to be realized. The sheep suffer much from the larvæ deposited by large flies in the wool all over the body of the animal, which devour it alive, and also from the penetrating barbed seeds of the coarse grass, which does not appear to be replaced by finer herbage, after being fed down or burned. It is possible, however, that both these evils may be overcome; but, judging from the condition of cattle as well as sheep, the natural grasses do not seem in the winter season to possess much nutriment. On the whole, it appears probable that the cultivation of cotton, and perhaps coffee and sugar, will be found to be the most profitable field for labour in the island, and the natives, when they have acquired a taste for European productions, may be made useful by the settlers.

# CHAPTER XVI.

## NORFOLK ISLAND.

*24th August.*—The weather during this week has been perfect, cool and calm; but we have made slow progress against the steady south-east trade, which we so much wished for on our passage to New Caledonia, when we had more reason to expect it to favour us. The barometer stands now at 30·50, promising us still more beating before we pass over the sixty miles between us and Norfolk Island. The Cape pigeons made their appearance in latitude 26° 30′, within half a degree of the parallel where we saw the last on our voyage to the north. The exactness with which sea-birds keep to the limits of their own proper cruising-ground is very singular.

*26th August.*—After two days' battling against a strong breeze, the "Fawn" backed her top-sail this afternoon, between Sydney Bay and the little island to which Governor Philip has given his name. It is the habitation of a multitude of rabbits, which have deprived it apparently of every vestige of vegetation, bearing only a high moundof red clay, with one or two pine-trees growing on it. The weather being squally and the wind fresh, the ship could not anchor, and stood off again for the night. John Adams, grandson of the patriarch of Pitcairns, having come off with a stout crew, the Captain, several of the officers, and myself, stowed ourselves in his boat,—our weight, with supplies for the islanders, bringing her nearly down to the water's edge, much too near indeed, to be pleasant. We had a long and wet pull to the landing-place, in a heavy, tumbling sea, which we reached just as daylight began to fade, drenched with spray. The surf was high and wild enough to-day, and boiled furiously off the rocky point, and across the entrance to the boat-harbour, in a manner that left no cause for surprise at the number of lives that have been lost in attempting to land here. We were met by the greater part of the population on the wharf, which, like everything here, is substantially built of well-cut stone. The prisoners' barracks and jails, the soldiers' barracks, and other public buildings, are on a large scale. The nearest building to the landing-place has a plain but handsome front; no ornamental carving is there; no escutcheons or pleasant devices, but on either side of the archway, let into the solid stone, are two pairs of ponderous leg-irons in saltire, and over the key-stone is a pair of veritable hand-cuffs, all *proper*, as the heralds would say,—significant, grim memorials of its former history.

Norfolk Island.

Much accustomed as we have been to hospitable receptions during the last few months, our welcome must have been a warm one to have been remarked by us at all. Our numbers were few, and the families numerous, and the great difficulty was how we were to be divided among them.

I accepted the invitation of the well-known Pastor of Pitcairns, to make his house my head-quarters during our stay. His history is a romantic one, and presents a fitting and curious parallel to that of the people whose instructor he has been for more than a quarter of a century, and of the islands now their peaceful abode. Originally a midshipman in the British Navy, he afterwards served under Lord Dundonald, and was in command of a boat at the famous cutting out of the frigate in the Basque Roads, surrounded with bombs, and under the muzzles of four hundred guns. He was twice a prisoner in the hands of the Chilians, when both sides showed no quarter, and under sentence of death, escaping on both occasions by the merest chance. After having worked in irons on the roads, and undergone many other strange vicissitudes, he at last finished the stormy life he had led for years by coming to be instructor of the Pitcairn Islanders, to whose isolated home he made his way, with one companion, in a little craft of twenty tons burden, after an adventurous voyage of three thousand five hundred miles. He has remained in happy relations with them ever since, with the exception of a period of nine months just thirty years ago, when he was obliged to leave, and take refuge in Lord Hood's Island, in consequence of the persecutions of an adventurer of the name of Hill. This person giving himself out to be a nephew of the Duke of Bedford, and stating that he had been sent out by the British Government to direct their affairs, managed to bring the simple islanders under his authority, and established a sort of reign of terror for a time, until the opportune arrival of Lord Edward Russell in H.M.S. "Actæon" put an end to his amusement, and Mr. Nobbs and his companions were sent for by their friends.

After visiting England, and being ordained a clergyman, he accompanied the community of Pitcairn Island, when removed by the British Government to this place, to spend the remainder of his days in peace and usefulness. This island, one of the loveliest spots on earth, is now occupied by perhaps the most moral and well-behaved community in existence, after having been for fifty years a blot upon the face of creation; the abode of criminals of the deepest dye, of whom endless tales might be recounted, which would serve but to make the flesh creep and the blood run cold. The sooner they are forgotten the better. One could not but feel a wish as we passed up the street, that the great prisons with their dismal emblems of punishment and their hundred dungeons were levelled with the ground, and every trace of the former history of Norfolk Island obliterated. As an example of the occurrences which were once common here, I will mention but one circumstance told me as we passed by a house on our way up, which was formerly the dispensary. An officer of one of the first ships of war which called here after the arrival of the Pitcairn Islanders, obtained thence a skull, the upper part of which had been completely cut off with an axe. On inquiry, this was found to be that of an overseer, himself a convict, who, whilst superintending a road gang, and leaning over a fence, received this fearful death-wound from one of the gang of prisoners, who committed the deed for the sole purpose of being sent to be tried in Sydney. The temporary change of scene to be obtained as the result of the crime was esteemed such a privilege, though an ignominious death was inevitable in a few weeks, that he had drawn lots with his comrade which should avail himself of the first opportunity to perpetrate the murder. So common did crimes become from this motive, that latterly all trials and executions took place on the island.

In the churchyard here I saw inscriptions such as are to be seen probably nowhere else. One row of grave-stones is there, each *sacred to the memory of* different individuals executed for mutiny, and another marked the resting-place of an old irreclaimable sinner, who died at the age of one hundred and five years, whilst undergoing his third sentence of transportation to this place. Amongst this host of villains, however, punishments and trials, severe as they doubtless were, appear in some few cases to have caused repentance, instead of hardening the heart, and to have brought out its latent good qualities, deadened perhaps from early childhood by misery and want; and it was pleasing to see one epitaph erected by the commanding officer, "to mark his deep sorrow" for the death of a convict servant.

There are several stones, I observed, lately placed in another portion of the cemetery, over the graves of the innocent race now occupying this gem in the Southern Ocean, who have met their deaths by accidents, nearly in every case by falls from horseback, which is not to be wondered at, considering the material used to caparison their ill-broken steeds. And in no other place have I seen recorded so many fatal results of boat accidents as are to be found here.

The story of the "Bounty" is an old one now,

and the perilous voyage of William Bligh her commander is well-nigh forgotten, although so deserving of remembrance as an instance of what may be accomplished by fortitude and resolution. Forty-one days in an open boat, with scarce provisions enough to sustain life, reduced to the twentieth part of a pound of food a day for each, he managed by his brave example and determined conduct, to bring his crew of eighteen souls all alive to Timor, after having endured almost unparalleled sufferings and privations during the voyage of nearly four thousand miles.

The fate of Christian his lieutenant, and those of the crew who left Tahiti in the ship which they had seized, A.D. 1790, remained unknown for many long years. In 1808, an American vessel, the "Topaz," touched at the island of Pitcairn, and the mate Folger reported the discovery of its inhabitants to the British Government, but no steps appear to have been taken in the matter, and in the excitement of the stormy times in Europe they seem to have been forgotten. On the 17th September 1814, Sir Thomas Staines, commanding H.M.S. "Britain," discovered, as he deemed it, an island not laid down in any chart, and hove-to till daylight, to ascertain whether it was inhabited.

Great must have been his surprise when a canoe came off, from which he was hailed in good English with, "Won't you heave us a rope now?" The request being quickly complied with, up jumped an athletic fine-looking young fellow, who hastened to shake hands with everybody in the most simple, warm-hearted manner, and made known his name as Thursday October Christian. The early history of the Pitcairn Islanders was dark and stormy, as the following extract from Sir Thomas Staines' letter to the Commander-in-Chief will suffice to show:—"They prove," he says, "to be the descendants of the deluded crew of the 'Bounty,' who from Otaheite proceeded to the above-mentioned island, where the ship was burnt. Christian the lieutenant appears to have been the leader and sole cause of the mutiny in that ship. A venerable old man named John Adams is the only surviving Englishman of those who last quitted Otaheite in her, and whose exemplary conduct and fatherly care of the whole of the little colony could not but command respect and admiration. The pious manner in which all those born in the island have been reared, the correct sense of religion which has been instilled into their young minds by this old man, have given him the pre-eminence over all, who look to him as the father of the whole, as one family. A son of Christian was the person born on the island, now about twenty-five years of age, named Thursday October Christian. The elder Christian fell a sacrifice to the jealousy of an Otaheite man within three or four years after their arrival on the island. They were accompanied thither by six Otaheite men and twelve women; the former were all swept away by desperate contentions between them, leaving only one man and seven women of the original settlers now alive."

Of the nine Englishmen—Adams, Christian, Young, MacCoy, Quintal, Brown, Martin, Mills, and Williams, several were killed by the Otaheitians, two died, and one was put to death by his countrymen, only two remaining alive in 1799, Young and Adams. The former died in 1800, leaving his sorrowing companion alone. Having become a very religious man, he devoted himself, heart and soul, to the instruction of the women and their numerous children, now all looking up to him as their father; and so well did he accomplish his task, that perhaps the world has never seen so virtuous, amiable, and religious a people as these islanders. Captain Beachey, who visited them in H.M.S. "Blossom" in 1825, says: "All that remains to be said of these excellent people is, that they appear to live together in perfect harmony and contentment; to be virtuous, religious, cheerful, and hospitable beyond the limits of prudence; to be a pattern of conjugal and parental affection, and to have no vices."

In 1830, the Hon. Captain Waldegrave, commanding H.M.S. "Seringapatam," paid them a visit, and expresses himself in similar terms: "It is with great satisfaction," he writes, "that I observed the Christian simplicity of their nature: they appear to have no guile. Their cottages are open to all, and all are welcome to their food. Before they began a meal, all joined hands in the attitude of prayer, with their eyes raised to heaven, and one recited a simple grace, each answering Amen. Should any one arrive during the repast, all ceased to eat, the new guest said grace, to which each repeated Amen, and the meal continued." So rigid were they in the performance of what they deemed to be correct, that for years every Wednesday and Friday were kept as strict fast-days. Old Adams (an entirely self-educated man, having taught himself to read after having reached Pitcairns), having observed the fast days of Ash Wednesday and Good Friday mentioned in the prayer-book, thought it right to observe these days in like manner every week, although the labour required daily to be undergone in order to provide the necessaries of life, was such that the starving labourers often fainted over their work from exhaustion. The effects of the precepts and example of this exemplary old man, who died revered and beloved, at the age of sixty-five, are not lost; and the children of his pupils are strict in the observance of their religious duties, as their parents were. Every morning at sunrise, there are prayers in every house, and grace is said in the same simple and earnest manner before all meals, as when Captain Waldegrave visited Pitcairns.

In 1831, their numbers being increased to eighty-seven, and the difficulty of providing a sufficient supply of food, and more especially water, in their little rocky island, which was little more than eight hundred acres in extent, becoming apparent, they were all removed at their own request in the "Lucy Ann" to Tahiti, under convoy of H.M.S. "Comet," Captain A. Sandilands. But disgusted with the levity and low morality of their Tahitian friends and relatives, and having been attacked with fever, which carried off twelve of their number, after a residence of nine months, they chartered a vessel, and returned to their former homes, curiously

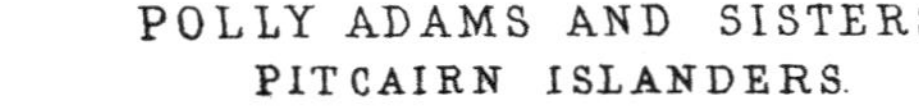

From a Photog by Commander R. P. Cator R.N.

W. & A. K. Johnston, Edinr

POLLY ADAMS AND SISTERS
PITCAIRN ISLANDERS.

enough paying great portion of the freight-money with the copper-bolts of the "Bounty."

In 1839, Captain Russell Eliott, in H.M.S. "Fly," visited the island, and reports finding "this interesting community preserving their deservedly high character for exemplary morality, innocence, and integrity." Hearing that they had been frequently annoyed by lawless strangers in whale-ships, who, taunting them with belonging to no country, and being under the protection of no flag, abused their hospitality, and in a late disturbance, "occasioned the concentration of the men's strength, for the personal protection of their females,"—Captain Eliott took possession of the island formally for the British Crown, gave the colony a Union Jack, and recognised Edward Quintal, the magistrate unanimously elected by the votes of all above the age of eighteen, both men and women, as responsible to the British Government for his proceedings. He drew up for them also a code of regulations, which were of the greatest use to these simple people, whose primitive state may be gathered from the quaint titles of some of them.

No. 1. was entitled Laws and Regulations for Pitcairn's Island.
,, 2. ,, Laws for Dogs.
,, 3. ,, Laws for Cats.

No. 4. was entitled Laws for Hogs.
,, 5. ,, Laws regarding the School.
,, 6. ,, Miscellaneous.
,, 7. ,, Laws for Trading with Ships.
,, 8. ,, Laws respecting Land Marks.
,, 9. ,, Laws for Wood.
,, 10. ,, Laws for the Public Anvil.

Some of the regulations not inserted in the code, but in daily use, are rather amusing, such as the following:—"If a fowl be seen trespassing in a garden, the proprietor may shoot and keep it, while the owner of the fowl shall return to him the powder and shot expended in killing it."

The young lovers being in the habit of carving each other's names with true-love knots, and such emblems, upon the soft stems of the plantains and bananas, "all carving upon trees or plants is forbidden." Both these regulations were of great importance, the latter practice injuring the plants which produced one of their staple articles of food; and the fowls having increased to such an extent, that gardens were much injured by their depredations. Some of these regulations are still retained in the code of laws drawn up for the islanders by Sir William Denison.[1]

From the time of Captain Eliott's useful visit,

[1] See Appendix, No. v.

all went on quietly, and even prosperously, many whalers calling for supplies, thirty having visited them in twelve months, affording them the opportunity of obtaining European productions, books, etc., in exchange for their surplus pigs. But the prospect for the future induced them again to petition Government in 1855 to grant them Norfolk Island, from which the penal establishment was about to be removed, where they might find more scope for the employment and subsistence of their fast increasing numbers; and in 1856, their petition having been acceded to, they left their well-loved little island, no doubt with many tears and regrets. The older people, who still look back to it with longing thoughts, speak of it with sighs and moistened eyelids, and two families have already returned, consisting chiefly of young girls; one of the matrons told me her husband had promised that four or five of his boys should go down, by and by, to marry their cousins, for all are more or less nearly related. Uncles and aunts are seen carried about in the arms of their nephews and nieces; and it will be a difficult matter by and by, for the genealogist of Norfolk Island, to make out a correct family tree.

They seem now generally happy, and reconciled to their new residence, which possesses many great advantages; and although here no cocoa-nut and bread-fruit trees shower their fruit down prodigally to earth, we may well say, O happy islanders! *sua si bona nôrint!* On the whole, we may consider that the removal of this interesting community to Norfolk Island has been a successful experiment; and it is satisfactory to see that the wise measures taken by Sir William Denison to induce them to be more energetic and industrious, have been productive of beneficial results.

It is difficult to imagine a state of society in which life flows more pleasantly on, though in an even tenor, than in the homes of these amiable people, by whom the troubles and turmoil of the world are heard only as the echo of far distant thunder. All being equal in fortune, prospects, and position, are free from the jealousies and heart-burnings which embitter the enjoyment of life to the most wealthy possessor of the seeming good things of this world. May it be long before the *auri sacra fames* disturbs the quiet of the little colony! Whaling seems the favourite occupation of the men, and galloping after their cattle. They have thus both sport and profitable employment, which they vary with work in their gardens and plantations, and now and then by a crusade against the rabbits in Philip's islands. The women find abundant means of passing their time, in attending to their dairies, and sewing for their numerous families. All are very fond of reading, and anxious to gather information from every source, of the world and its history. Some are very well informed indeed. I made the acquaintance of one of the daughters of the first generation, whose knowledge of the manners and customs of different people, and the geography of their countries, was remarkably extensive. They have the advantage in this respect of their good fathers and mothers, who, when young, knew their Bible well, but nothing else. Only two of the men of the first generation are now living, Adams and Quintal. The latter, a quaint old man, told us that when he was a boy, playing with his companions early one morning on the beach, he was startled, like Robinson Crusoe with the footprints, by finding a big jack-knife on the shore, and seeing a number of branches of cocoa-nut trees freshly cut. Looking around, they espied a large strange object on the ocean; and running home, learned from their father, old Adams, that it was a ship. They remained under the idea for a long time (for perhaps he thought it better not to instruct them in anything regarding the outer world) that it had come through the hole in the horizon where the sun rose. This was the first sail seen by them, and was probably some whale-ship, whose crew, after helping themselves to the nuts, made all haste to be off from an island inhabited they thought probably by savages, as, small and isolated though it be, it once was, by what race however is unknown. Stone axes and other implements are found frequently ; and upon a rock on the shore are cut a number of hieroglyphics resembling those upon the famous inscriptive rock in the Zunis Valley of North America. Human skeletons of very large dimensions have been seen by my informant, dug up at various times from under tumuli of stones. Old Adams seems indeed to have thought of nothing but to teach his people to do justly and walk uprightly ; and it must have somewhat amused the people in the first ship that had communication with them, when explaining that they had sailed round the world, to be met by the rejoinder from a grown up man,—"Round the world! I can go round the world in two hours," the circumference of Pitcairns being three miles and a half.

All, both old and young, seem passionately fond of music. They have a singing class every Wednesday ; and we listened with great pleasure to the glees and sacred music performed in good time. Both men and women appear to have full, rich-toned voices; and they certainly do great credit to Mr. Carleton, a gentleman well known in New Zealand, who, during an accidental detention at Pitcairns, instructed them in music. Their love of dancing, inherited from their Otaheitian mothers, is as great as that of the girls of Spain. They are bold riders; and in our expeditions we were accompanied by a number of fair equestrians, who galloped along in a way that made one feel rather nervous for their safety, holding on in some mysterious manner without any crutch, on common saddles.

Norfolk Island, from the sea, looks rather bare, its coast being iron-bound; in places the high cliffs are composed of fine basaltic pillars. It is quite unapproachable for boats even, except at Sydney Bay, and opposite another sloping part of the coast, called the Cascades, on the other side of the island. The extreme and peculiar beauty of its scenery is all the more charming and surprising. Although not possessing the exuberant luxuriance of the tropical vegetation, it is indeed a most lovely island. The hills and valleys are clothed with rich grass, and shaded with forests, groves, and single individuals of the magnificent Norfolk Island Pine (*Araucaria excelsa*), disposed as if by the hands of the landscape gardener, in the most picturesque manner over the whole island, up to the top of Mount Pitt, which rises to the height of more than a thousand feet. It resembles one grand park. There is one avenue of these trees a mile and a half in length, which is unequalled in beauty by anything of the kind I have ever seen. At right angles it is crossed by another road, passing between two rows of splendid tree-ferns, the effect of which is almost as pleasing as that of the avenue of cocoanut trees at Wallis Island.

The present inhabitants have to thank one of the former Commandants, whose good taste has so much added to the delightful landscape. Some of these pines, which have flourished for ages on the slopes of Mount Pitt, are most noble trees, from thirty to forty feet in circumference, and more than two hundred in height. Sheep and cattle, sleek and comfortable-looking, are seen in all directions revelling in the abundant pasture; and wild turkeys, fowls, and pigs, find luxurious abodes under the shelter of the thick groves of Guava, Lemon, and Loquat trees, from which one disturbs large flocks of pigeons, the descendants of the imported dove-cote breed, which are not now distinguishable from the blue-rock. There is also a large indigenous spècies, which is the only bird peculiar to the place worth mentioning, excepting the curious wingless parrot in Philip Island, now extinct.

The description I have given may seem *couleur de rose;* but those who have seen Norfolk Island in a bright, calm day, will think it gives but a meagre idea of its quiet beauty. We have passed our time very pleasantly on the island, and every one feels a deep interest in the welfare of its warm-hearted inhabitants. We are to take as passengers their late chief magistrate, Frederic Young, elected by the unanimous votes of the community (for universal suffrage is carried out to an extent which would delight American ladies, every individual above the age of eighteen having a vote), and his little boy, *Alfred Denison,* about five years old, whom the islanders begged Commander Cator to take to Sydney, in order to have an operation performed on his eyes, there being no medical man on the island. His father goes to see Sir John Young, the Governor of New South Wales (under whose jurisdiction the little colony is placed), regarding two matters of great importance to its prosperity. No one is allowed to land upon the island without the approbation of the acting magistrate, and the consent of the Governor. It appears that the number of marriageable females considerably exceeds that of the young men, so there are now somewhere about twenty doomed to celibacy, unless some young fellows, induced by feelings of gallantry, and the wedding-portion of fifty acres of land, are permitted by his Excellency to take pity upon their hopeless condition, and settle upon the island.

A very similarly constituted little colony is rising at Lord Howe's Island, a few days' sail from the abode of the Pitcairn islanders. A few weeks ago, a young man and his bride-elect came up in a whale-ship to be married by the pastor of Norfolk Island; these people are the children and grandchildren of two respectable Englishmen, who settled on this solitary mountain in mid ocean. It is probable, from what we heard, that some of the forlorn damsels on the larger island may find suitors from thence, now that the knowledge of their existence, and the fame of their beauty has reached its wooded shores. But meantime it will be very desirable, for many reasons, that Young should be successful in his mission, and meet with some well-behaved artisans, willing to make their home in this lovely island, who would be also of great service in teaching the people various useful trades. The other matter is also one in which it seems to me it would be very desirable that the wishes of the islanders should be complied with: the cattle and sheep on the island are still considered the property of Her Majesty's Government; their produce, certainly, is entirely devoted to the benefit of the community, but the management of the stock, and the fund derived therefrom, is under the control of Mr. Rossiter, the schoolmaster, sent from England upon Sir William Denison's recommendation.

Disagreeable feelings are very likely soon to arise between him and the people in consequence, which will much impair his usefulness; besides, they take now very little interest in the management of the stock, which no doubt they would do, did they consider them actually their own; and the result is that the sheep are in a very unhealthy state, which is much to be regretted, as with attention they might become a valuable property, quite sufficient, in the course of a few years, to produce an export of sufficient value to pay for all foreign necessaries for a considerable population; the cattle are also becoming much too numerous, and are very wild, indeed positively dangerous.

The success of their envoy to Sydney is anxiously

looked forward to by all, old and young, who accompanied us in a body, with sorrowful looks, to Cascade Bay, where the "Fawn" lay at anchor. After a dance, which checked for a time the tears which plentifully rolled down their cheeks, they bade us good-bye, taking a most affectionate farewell of their relatives; each one presenting something by way of a remembrance, and the joint community a bag, containing all the gold I should suppose in their possession, to pay for the medical advice and the expenses in a *distant* foreign land, which demonstration of affection quite overcame their friend.

The anchor being weighed, the boats at last reluctantly pushed off, and we bore away on the evening of 31st August for Sydney, where, after a very fine passage, we arrived on the 2d September 1862.

The sailors, of course, made a great pet of little Alfred, who soon appeared on the deck in full costume as a miniature man-of-war's man, which it is his father's ambition he shall be, the British navy being the object of most ardent veneration and affection with every Pitcairn Islander.

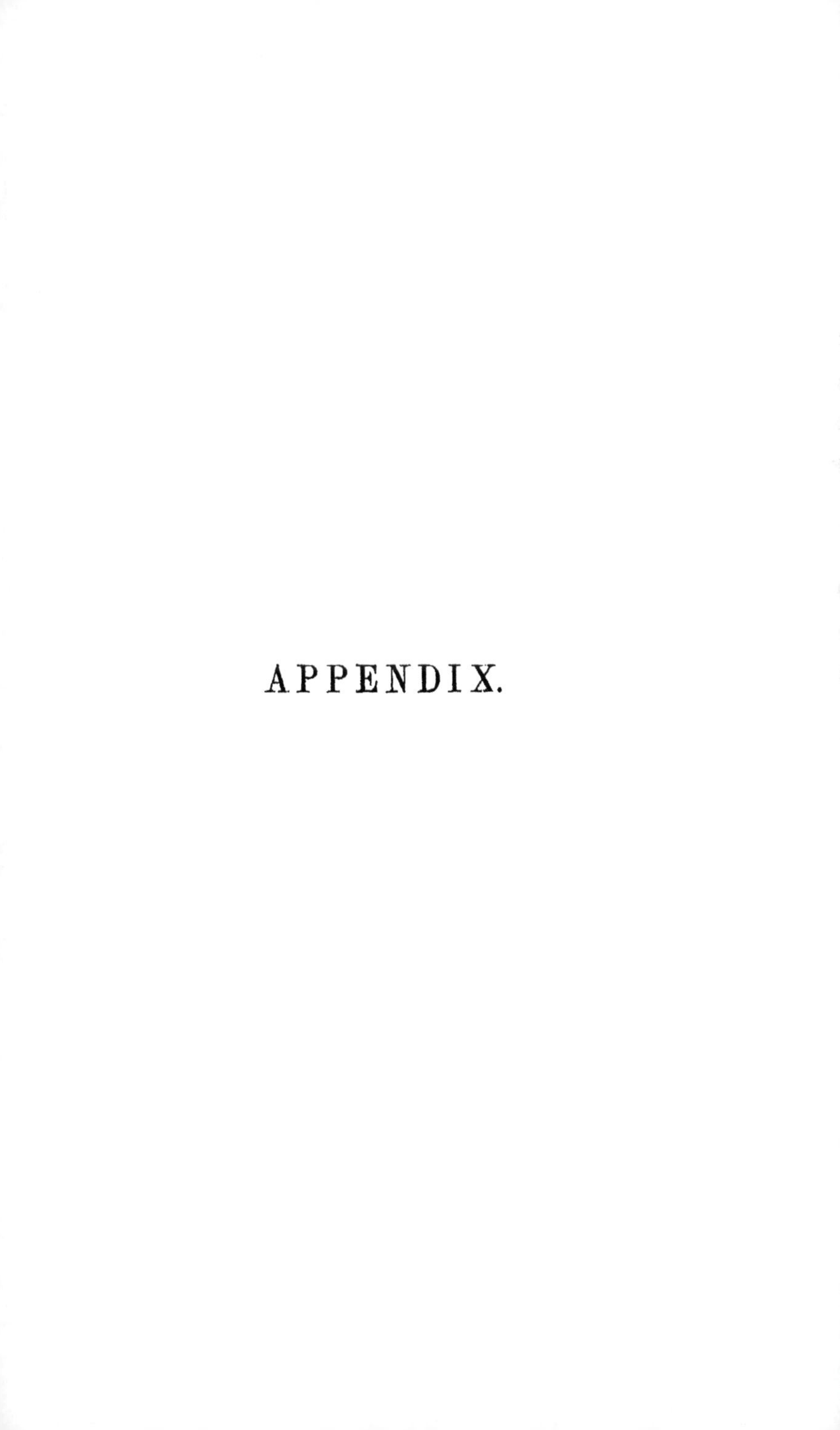

# APPENDIX.

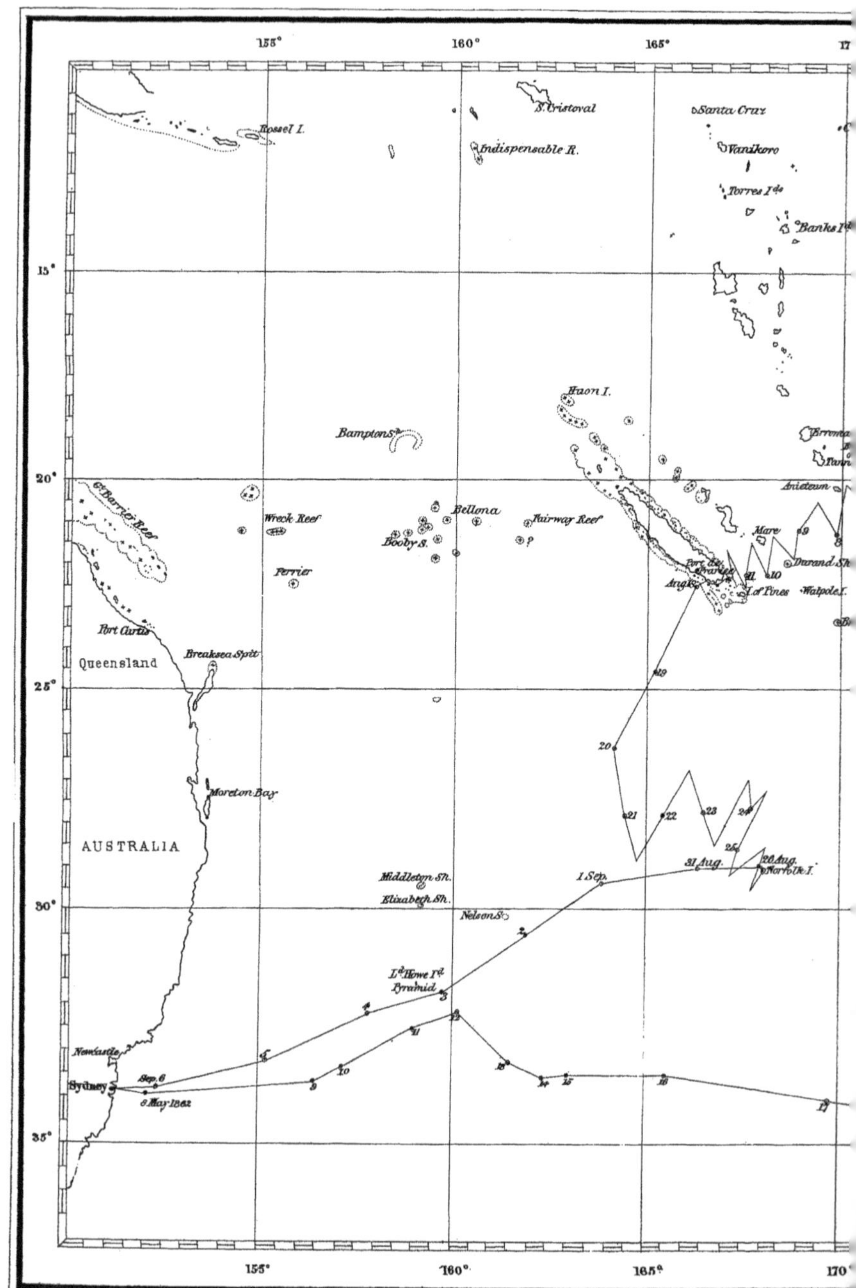
155°
160°
165°
15°
20°
25°
30°
35°
170°
Rossel I.
S. Cristoval
Santa Cruz
Vanikoro
Indispensable R.
Torres Ids
Banks Id
Huon I.
Bamptons
Erromanga
Tanna
Anieteum
Barrier Reef
Wreck Reef
Bellona
Fairway Reef
Booby S.
Mare
Durand Sh.
Ferrier
Port de France
I. of Pines
Walpole I.
Port Curtis
Breaksea Spit
Queensland
Moreton Bay
AUSTRALIA
Middleton Sh.
Elizabeth Sh.
Nelson S.
1 Sep.
31 Aug.
20 Aug.
Norfolk I.
Ld Howe Id
Pyramid
Newcastle
Sydney
Sep. 6
8 May 1862

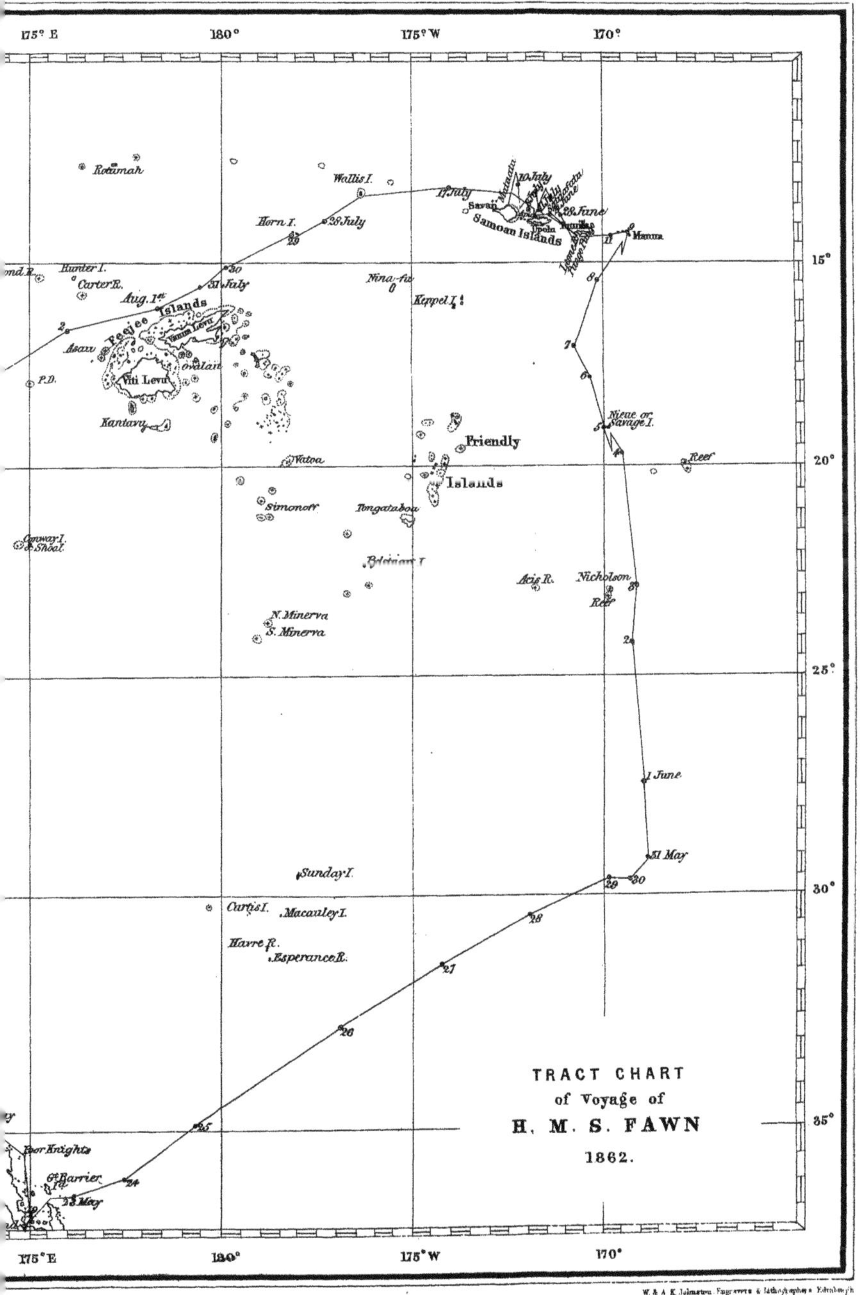

175° E
180°
175° W
170°
15°
20°
25°
30°
35°
Rotumah
Wallis I.
Horn I.
28 July
17 July
10 July
28 June
Savaii
Samoan Islands
Upolu
Manua
Hunter I.
Carter R.
31 July
Aug. 1st
Feejee Islands
Vanua Levu
Viti Levu
Ovalau
Kantavu
P.D.
Nina-fu
Keppel I.
Niue or Savage I.
Friendly Islands
Reef
Vatoa
Simonoff
Tongataboa
Conway I. & Shoal
Acis R.
Nicholson Reef
N. Minerva
S. Minerva
1 June
31 May
Sunday I.
Curtis I.
Macauley I.
Havre R.
Esperance R.
Poor Knights
Gt. Barrier Id.
23 May
TRACT CHART
of Voyage of
H. M. S. FAWN
1862.
W. & A. K. Johnston, Engravers & Lithographers, Edinburgh

# APPENDIX.

## No. I., p. 8.

It is to be hoped that ere long we shall have another work added to the number, by the gentlemen now engaged in the Geological Survey of the Middle Island. The examination of the deposits upon both flanks of the lofty Cordillera, will be highly interesting. Many persons have entertained hopes that certain theories will have evidence produced in their favour, when the unknown leaves of the Stone Book are opened, which at the antipodes may have escaped destruction by the cataclysms that elsewhere destroyed them; and that there we may find traces of transitional forms displayed to view. It may be so; but, so far as we have yet seen, these expectations are little likely to be realized. The discovery, by the writer, of Mesozoic deposits, containing the remains of Saurians similar in form to those of like age in Europe and elsewhere, and overlaid by equivalent formations, seems to point to a very different conclusion.

On the Remains of a Plesiosaurian Reptile (*Plesiosaurus Australis*) from the Oolitic Formation in the Middle Island of New Zealand. By Professor Owen, M.D., F.R.S., F.G.S.

The author, premising a quotation from his *Palæontology*, that "the further we penetrate into time, for the recovery of extinct animals, the further we must go into space to find their existing analogues;" and that, "in passing from the more recent to the older strata, we soon obtain indications of extensive changes in the relative position of land and sea," cited some striking examples in proof of these propositions from the reptilian class. The Mosasaurus of the Cretaceous series occurs in that series in England, Germany, and the United States. The Polyptzchodon occurs in the same series at Maidstone and at Moscow. Toothless lacertian reptiles have left their remains in Triassic deposits at Elgin, in Shropshire, and at the Cape of Good Hope. Dicynodont reptiles occur in the same formation at the Cape and in Bengal. The Plesiosaurus, with a more extensive geological range through the Triassic or Oolitic series, has left representatives of its genus in those Mesozoic strata in England and at her antipodes. Evidence of this extreme of geographical range has been submitted to Professor Owen, by Mr. T. H. Hood, F.G.S., of Queensland, obtained by him from the Middle Island of New Zealand. This evidence consists of two vertebral bodies or centrums, ribs, and portions of the two coracoids of the same individual, all in the usual petrified condition of oolitic fossils. Their matrix was a bluish-grey claystone, effervescing with acid. The largest mass contained impressions of parts of the arch and of the transverse processes of nine dorsal vertebræ, and of ten ribs of the right side. Portions of five of the right diapophyses and of six of the ribs remained in this matrix. The bones had a ferruginous tint, contrasting with the matrix, as is commonly the case with specimens imbedded in the Oxfordian or Liassic clays. The impression of the first diapophysis, and of its ribs, shows the latter to have been articulated by a simple head to its extremity, as in the Plesiosaurus; but the succeeding rib had been pushed a little behind the end of its diapophysis, and the same kind of dislocation had placed the five following ribs with their articular ends opposite the interspaces of their diapophyses. The ninth rib had nearly resumed its proper position opposite the end of the diapophysis, but at some distance from it. The impression of the tenth rib shows the normal relative position of the pleurand diapophyses. The ribs are solid, of compact texture, cylindrical, slightly curved, the fragments looking more like coprolite than bone. They are about one inch in diameter, but with small intervals of, say, one third of an inch, slightly expanding as they recede from the transverse process, and slightly contracting to the lower end. The first, terminating in an obtuse end of half an inch diameter, is seven inches long ; the second is eight inches long ; the third is eight and a half inches ; the fourth rib is nine inches long. The extremities of the others are broken off with the matrix. The separated fossils sent from New Zealand, included the mesial coadjusted ends of a pair of long and broad bones, thickest where they were united, and becoming thinner as they extended outwards, and also towards the fore and hind parts of the bone, both of which were broken away. On one side the surface of the bone is convex lengthwise, and slightly concave transversely. On the opposite side, the contour undulates lengthwise, the surface being concave, then rising to a convexity, where a protuberance has been formed by part of the coadjusted mesial margins of the bone ; transversely this surface is slightly concave. A similar, but less developed median prominence is seen at the middle of the medially united margins of the coracoids in the *Plesiosaurus Hawkinsii*, and the author regards the above described parts of the New Zealand fossils as being homologous bones. But a more decided evidence of the plesiosaurian nature of this antipodal fossil, is afforded by the vertebral centrums. They have flat articular ends, with two large and two small venous foramina beneath. The neurapophysial surfaces, showing the persistent independence of the neural arch, are separated from the costal surfaces by about half the diameter of the latter. These are of a full oval figure, one inch three lines in vertical, and one inch in fore and aft diameter. On one side of one of the centrums, the rib has coalesced with the costal surface. The following are the dimensions of this centrum :—length, one inch nine lines ; depth, two inches two lines ; breadth of auricular end, three inches six lines. The non-auricular part of the centrum offers a fine silky character. The shape and mode of articulation of the cervical and dorsal ribs, the shape and proportion of the coracoids, concur with the more decisive evidence of the vertebræ, in attesting the plesiosauroid character of these New Zealand fossils; and, pending the discovery of the teeth, the author provisionally referred them to a species, for which he proposed the name *Plesiosaurus Australis.* The specimen had been presented by Mr. Hood to the British Museum.

## No. II., p. 22.

THE treatment of females alluded to is so extraordinary, that I am induced to mention it, if only to show what human beings in a state of nature can survive. I was informed by the clergyman, that the practice described below was at one time invariable amongst them: 'Mulieres statim ut pepererunt, ab iis quæ partui intersint, capite prono elevantur. Deinde ubi vacuus uterus aquâ salsâ per calamum injectâ impletus est, puerperæ ingenti vi huc illuc commoventur.' The deaths resulting from this severe usage are singularly few.

## No. III., p. 187.

IT is to be feared that the practice of cannibalism has not diminished, as generally believed, of late years, amongst the Fijians, except in the principal resorts of Europeans, or in the neighbourhood of missionary stations. I was informed by a gentleman, who had just returned from the islands after a sojourn of a year (during which he attempted to grow cotton with native servants, but unsuccessfully, in consequence of their unwillingness to engage in regular labour), that in the part of the island where he resided there was a considerable village, in which he discovered, shortly before leaving, when his own people had become communicative and familiar, that, on the average, four or five unfortunates, stolen from neighbouring districts, were weekly sacrificed to satisfy the craving for this horrible food; not from necessity, for they have fish, fruit, and pigs in abundance. On one occasion, his own servant came back, after a lengthened absence, in a state of hilarious excitement, and, being questioned, admitted that he had returned from being a partaker in a terrible banquet. The victim being a girl of tender years, had not even been placed in the oven, but devoured as soon as slain. Thakombau, the most powerful chief in the group, who pretends to be a Christian now, and behaved on board Admiral Erskine's ship with the dignity and good manners of an Indian noble, went not long ago to visit one of his more remote districts. On landing from his war canoe, with conches blowing and guns saluting, he walked up between two rows of people of both sexes, some grown up, others mere children, suspended by their feet, and touched with his club those whom he wished first to be killed. But this man bears, even amongst his own countrymen, the reputation of being superlatively cruel, where all seem to delight in giving pain. Even the girls in their dances have head-dresses of live fire-flies, which they impale upon slips of bamboo, and manage to fix in such a manner, that for hours their coronets coruscate with the flashes from these living diamonds.

One cannot regret that this people are now seemingly

bent upon the extinction of their own race. Of late years the use of a preparation from a poisonous root, which causes sterility, is becoming very common.

## No. IV., p. 193.

Tokilau, as the natives in their happy ignorance call it, means the great land. It is a remarkable one, from all accounts, being described by the Rev. Mr. Turner as the most singularly beautiful and romantic spot in the South Seas. The people are good-looking, he says, and of a gentle disposition, very industrious and ingenious. They have no stone in all their extensive territory wherewith to make their hatchets, and use shells instead, hollowing their canoes slowly by fire. Some of their traditions and mythological fables are curious. They worship the Tui-Tokilau, or the King of Tokilau, whose spiritual embodiment is in a certain stone always kept carefully wrapped up in fine mats, like the stone idol of the ancient Irish. They believe that the first man had his origin from a small stone at Fakea-fo, and that after a time living on earth in solitude, he bethought himself it would be well to try and make himself a companion. He made the head, arms, legs, and body of clay, then taking a rib from his own side, he thrust it into the model, which suddenly jumped up on its feet a living woman, whom he called Ivi or Eevee.

No fire must burn at night, so they sit and talk in the dark. An adventurous individual named Talanga first obtained for them this element, having gone down to the lower regions, and got it there from an old woman named Mafuike, who querulously refused it for a long time, but at last, compelled by threats of death, yielded up a portion of her treasure, part of which Talanga enclosed in a particular kind of tree, from the wood of which they now obtain it by friction.

Some, when about to die, say to their friends, "I'm going to be a star," or "I intend going to the moon." More affectionate people say to their relatives, "I shan't go away far. I will remain in my grave, and be here with you."

## No. V., p. 240.

INSTRUCTIONS and ADVICE addressed to the Chief Magistrate of Norfolk Island by Sir W. Denison, Governor-General of Australia.

The object of Her Majesty's Government, in transferring the Pitcairn islanders to their present residence, were, first, to put them in a position to maintain their increasing numbers by their own industry, and, second, to enable them to keep up, so far as the change of circumstances may permit, the peculiar form of polity under which they have hitherto existed as a community.

It will therefore be the duty of the chief magistrate, while administering the affairs of the Colony, during the absence of the Governor, to keep these two objects steadily in view; to see that the labour of the islanders is properly applied to the cultivation of the ground; that a sufficient area is brought under cultivation to supply all the probable wants of the community, so that it may not be necessary to purchase flour or biscuit from the adjacent Colonies, and while doing this, to be careful not to sanction any deviation from the principles which, by maintaining a sort of family feeling among the whole of the community, have enabled them to live together in peace and harmony up to the present time.

The rules and regulations which have been submitted by me for the consideration of the community, and have now been issued under the authority vested in me by Her Majesty, have been framed in strict accordance with those under which your affairs have hitherto been administered. Some few rules have been abrogated, as having no relation to the state of things now existing, and one or two have been added to provide for circumstances contingent upon the position of Norfolk Island, in the immediate vicinity of the Colonies of Australia and New Zealand.

I allude specially to the rule which prohibits the introduction upon the island of spirituous or fermented liquors, except for purposes purely medicinal. The evils which are forced daily upon my notice as originating from the use, and consequent abuse of these stimulants, are too great not to make me most anxious to guarantee, if possible, the inhabitants of Norfolk Island from them; and as none among you have ever been accustomed to the use of these stimulants, it can be no possible hardship that you should be prevented by legal enactment from indulging a taste which experience shows does too often lead to crime and to sin.

It must, however, be obvious to every one, that the very altered position in which you are now placed, must eventually render obligatory many additions to these regulations. Nothing has been said as yet with relation to the alienation of land by the Crown, and its transference to individual proprietors ; nothing to regulate the admission upon the island of settlers who may wish to become members of your community; nothing to indicate the mode in which the descent of property from parents to children is to be hereafter regulated, etc. etc. These, with several others, are matters which you have hitherto had little occasion to consider. They are questions, however, which will soon be forced upon your attention. They ought not, however, to be hastily dealt with, or be subjected to the operation of any arbitrary rule, the object of which you might be incapable of comprehending. I have therefore left them untouched for the present, in order that they might be submitted hereafter to the deliberate consideration of the people themselves, guided only by such advice as the Governor, from his position, and from the more extended means of information at his disposal, may be qualified to give.

Some advice, upon matters of special interest to the community, I shall now give, and I shall accompany this with such positive instructions to the chief magistrate as may tend to facilitate several of the arrangements which must very shortly be made.

The present state of matters on Norfolk Island is, I believe, altogether incompatible with its prosperity, or with the comfort and happiness of the people. You appear to be living, not on the produce of your own labour, but upon your capital, or rather upon that capital which was handed over to you by the Government for the purpose of being employed reproductively for your own benefit and that of your posterity. The scabby state of the sheep, and the impossibility of dressing them properly, may be a sufficient reason for killing them off gradually; but unless steps are soon taken to introduce more of this stock, and for allowing the cattle to increase, the supply of animal food will soon fall short of the wants of the people.

The habit which you are acquiring of depending for a large portion of your food upon a source which is entirely independent of any exertion of your own, must manifestly lead to the introduction of improvident and idle habits which cannot be too carefully guarded against. The first thing, therefore, to be done, is to make a positive and marked distinction between public and private property; to give to each head of a family an absolute right of property in a certain amount of land, and to make him a present of a sufficient number of cattle, etc., to enable him to cultivate that land with advantage, supposing him to exercise the ordinary amount of forethought and industry.

When this has been done, an end should be put at once and for ever to any gratuitous distributions of food, clothing, etc., from public funds, except perhaps to those who, from age, infirmity, and mental or bodily incapacity, are unable to maintain themselves.

In order to pave the way for this important change, the chief magistrate will arrange with the heads of families, and with those unmarried persons who may wish to acquire property of their own, for the selection by each of such an amount of land, not in any case exceeding fifty acres, in such a position as may seem to them most advantageous. A rough approximation to the area of a land may be made by stepping round it, and the following table will give the number of paces, each pace being taken at thirty inches, which it will take to include certain areas :—

| Area in Acres. | No. of Paces in Circumference. | No. of Paces in each Side of Square. |
|---|---|---|
| 10 Acres, . . . . | 1026 | 256 |
| 20 „ . . . . | 1450 | 368 |
| 30 „ . . . . | 1780 | 445 |
| 40 „ . . . . | 2053 | 513 |
| 50 „ . . . . | 2296 | 569 |

Marks should be placed at the corner of these allotments, and I will send properly qualified persons to make the necessary surveys and plans of the different properties from which the formal grants will be drawn up and issued by me in pursuance of the powers vested in me by Her Majesty. Looking, however, to the object which, as I have before stated, the Government had in view in removing the present occupants from Pitcairn to Norfolk Island, I do not think that the grant in fee-simple to the settler should be altogether unconditional. I do not think that it would be desirable to allow the settler to sell the land to persons unconnected with the island. Should any one wish to leave the island, his property should be first offered to individual inhabitants, and should none be willing to purchase it, the community might be empowered to do so at a valuation.

When the allotments of land have been selected, the following articles may be handed over to each occupant:

1*st.* A certain number of cattle, sheep, pigs, poultry, etc.

2*d.* Such tools and implements as may be necessary to enable him to cultivate the land.

3*d.* Such an amount of corn, potatoes, etc. etc., as may be necessary to enable him to plant a sufficient area to maintain his family.

The amount of stock should not be too great; a cow or an ox to every ten acres, will, I think, be ample.

Each proprietor will put a mark upon his own stock, to enable him to distinguish it from that of his neighbour, and from that of the public, and these marks should be notified to the chief magistrate, and recorded by him, and when once established, should not be allowed to be modified or altered.

The stock of individual proprietors may be allowed to run upon the unallotted parts of the island for the present; but as it is evident that this unallotted portion will rapidly diminish as fresh families take up grants of land, it will be necessary that each proprietor should take early steps to fence in his own land, and to divide it off in such a manner as will enable him to keep his own stock on his own ground.

It is the more necessary that this should be done, as the manure made by the stock will ultimately be required for the proper cultivation of the soil. At present, this is very rich; but each proprietor will act wisely in looking forward to the period when, in order to obtain proper crops, it will be necessary to apply manure, and in commencing to collect manure for that purpose at once.

When the land, and a proper amount of stock, has been handed over to different individuals, it must be distinctly understood that nothing is to be drawn by any one from the public store for his private use, without payment for the same at its full market price.

As no individual settler is in a position to establish a store, it is necessary that a public store should be maintained, at which clothing, stores, tools, etc., should be kept for sale, a fixed price being placed upon each article, so that every person may know what he will have to pay.

The establishment of a store will entail the appointment of a storekeeper, to whom the charge of all public stores of every kind will be handed over, and who will be held accountable for them. He will have to keep an account against each individual settler, crediting him with any payments, either in money, stock, or produce, and debiting him with the cost of any article which he may have purchased from the store.

The storekeeper may also be the schoolmaster; the salary which he will receive for the performance of these duties, together with the contingent advantages, will probably be sufficient to enable the community to secure the services of a competent person.

I have said that the chief magistrate should see that the labour of the islanders is properly applied to the cultivation of the ground.

It appears to me, that in order to place the community in a position to feed themselves, without reference to the adjacent colonies, at least eighty acres of maize should be planted; and, looking to the calls which may be made upon this crop for other purposes, it would be better to plant 100 acres of maize, irrespective of the land appropriated to the growth of potatoes, yams, bananas, and other vegetable products. If then such an amount of land has to be brought under cultivation, the labour of every member of the community should be rendered available toward it, and some check should be imposed upon the prolonged absence of those who, by going away from the island for a time, during the preparation of the ground for a crop, do, in point of fact, compel others to do their work. When once the land is given over to individuals, then any check of this kind will be unnecessary, but till then it should be imposed.

The present mode of working the ground with the hoe is both dilatory and unsatisfactory; it would be as well, as soon as possible, to introduce the use of the plough; until this is done, the labour of a large portion of the adult inhabitants will be expended in the production of food, leaving but little available for the cultivation of articles which will be useful to exchange for the products of other countries.

I am not aware, however, that there is any person on the island who knows how to use a plough. In the same way, the islanders are now placed in possession of buildings constructed of stone and plastered within and without, yet they are not in a position to carry out any repairs of these houses, as they know not how to burn lime, to make mortar, to plaster walls and ceilings, etc. In fact, there are several trades which ought, for the comfort and convenience of the inhabitants, to be practised on the island, but of which the present settlers are ignorant.

They have water and windmills, yet, for want of a competent millwright and smith, they must grind their corn in handmills; how then can those immediate and prospective wants be adequately supplied?

With regard to the millwright and smith, I do not think it at all improbable that a competent person might be induced to settle upon the island, by the grant of the water and windmill, subject to a condition that he would grind all the corn of the community at a fixed rate, that is, as in Canada, at a fixed proportion of the quantity brought to the mill, say one-twelfth; the same person would be qualified to act as smith, for the repair of tools, etc. etc., and as wheelwright. Were a circular saw attached to the mill-wheel, all the timber required for the use of the community might be cut up at a cheap rate.

For the repair of the houses a mason and plasterer will be required, and a shoemaker is very much wanted. It may be possible to induce a few persons of this stamp to settle on the island; but beyond these, whose services may be said to be actually indispensable to the comfort and welfare of the inhabitants, I should not be disposed to admit of the introduction of any strangers.

Pending then the establishment of some rule as regards this, the chief magistrate will understand that he is not to permit strangers to remain on the island, or to occupy, except for a short visit, any of the public buildings. There is one point which it is advisable to bring at once under the notice of the people, not with a view to any immediate action, but for the purpose of carefully considering the course which it may hereafter be desirable to adopt.

Hitherto the public funds have been adequate to supply the wants of the community; the sale of wool, tallow, live stock, etc., has produced a sum sufficient to cover the expense of purchasing flour, clothing, etc., but this source of revenue will very soon be dried up, and it will be necessary to devise some mode in which these expenses, which are properly chargeable upon the general fund of the community (which expenses must annually increase), may be adequately provided for, I mean such expenses as payment to the chaplain, to the storekeeper, the maintenance of roads and public buildings, the salary of the chief magistrate, etc. etc. There are several modes in which this may be done, but I am disposed to think, looking to the peculiar constitution of the society, that the best mode would be to tithe the produce of every kind, and thus to create one fund upon which all these payments would be chargeable.

These are the principal suggestions which I have to make at present, and I do not think that any positive instructions, save those embodied in this paper, will be required by the chief magistrate; I will conclude then by assuring the islanders of the affectionate interest I take in their welfare, and by praying them to remember that all the blessings which they have received are God's gift, and are to be employed in His service, not necessarily by any special dedication of them, but by striving in everything to do His will and to walk in His way.

(Signed) W. Denison.

EDINBURGH: T. CONSTABLE,
PRINTER TO THE QUEEN, AND TO THE UNIVERSITY.

www.ingramcontent.com/pod-product-compliance
Ingram Content Group UK Ltd.
Pitfield, Milton Keynes, MK11 3LW, UK
UKHW020415250726
13967UKWH00007B/2650